On
Courage

What is courage and why is it one of the oldest and most universally admired virtues? How is it relevant in the world today, and what contemporary forms does it take? What is the difference between physical and moral courage, and is it rightly portrayed as a "manly" virtue?

In this insightful and crisply written book, Geoffrey Scarre examines these questions and many more. He begins by defining courage, asking how it differs from fearlessness, recklessness and fortitude, and why people are often more willing to ascribe it to others than to avow it for themselves. He also asks whether courage can serve bad ends as well as good and whether it can sometimes promote confrontation over compromise and dialogue.

On Courage explores the ideas of Aristotle, Aquinas and many later philosophers who have written about courage, as well as drawing on classic and recent examples of courage in politics and fiction, including the German anti-Nazi "White Rose" movement, the modern phenomenon of "whistle-blowing", and Stephen Crane's The Red Badge of Courage.

An inspiring defence of courage and its value in the contemporary world, On Courage is essential reading for anyone interested in what philosophy has to say about this most popular of virtues.

Geoffrey Scarre is a Professor of Philosophy at Durham University, UK. His main research interests are in moral philosophy, and he is author of the Routledge book Utilitarianism (1996) and Death (2007).

Thinking in Action

Series editors: Simon Critchley, *The New School University, New York*, and Richard Kearney, *Boston College, USA*, and *University College Dublin*

Thinking in Action is a major new series that takes philosophy to its public. Each book in the series is written by a major international philosopher or thinker, engages with an important contemporary topic, and is clearly and accessibly written. The series informs and sharpens debate on issues as wide ranging as the Internet, religion, the problem of immigration and refugees, criticism, architecture, and the way we think about science. Punchy, short and stimulating, **Thinking in Action** is an indispensable starting point for anyone who wants to think seriously about major issues confronting us today.

Praise for the series

"... allows a space for distinguished thinkers to write about their passions."
The Philosophers' Magazine

"... deserve high praise."
Boyd Tonkin, *The Independent* (UK)

"This is clearly an important series. I look forward to receiving future volumes."
Frank Kermode, author of *Shakespeare's Language*

"both rigorous and accessible."
Humanist News

"the series looks superb."
Quentin Skinner

"... an excellent and beautiful series."
Ben Rogers, author of *A.J. Ayer: A Life*

"Routledge's Thinking in Action series is the theory junkie's answer to the eminently pocketable Penguin 60s series."
Mute Magazine (UK)

"Routledge's new series, *Thinking in Action*, brings philosophers to our aid...."
The Evening Standard (UK)

"... a welcome series by Routledge."
Bulletin of Science, Technology and Society (Can)

"Routledge's innovative new 'Thinking in Action' series takes the concept of philosophy a step further."
The Bookwatch

GEOFFREY SCARRE

On
Courage

Routledge
Taylor & Francis Group

LONDON AND NEW YORK

First published 2010
by Routledge
2 Park Square, Milton Park, Abingdon, Oxon OX14 4RN

Simultaneously published in the USA and Canada
by Routledge
270 Madison Avenue, New York, NY 10016

Routledge is an imprint of the Taylor & Francis Group, an informa business

© 2010 Geoffrey Scarre

Typeset in Joanna MT and Din by
RefineCatch Ltd, Bungay, Suffolk
Printed and bound in Great Britain by
TJ International Ltd, Padstow, Cornwall

British Library Cataloguing in Publication Data
A catalogue record for this book is available from the British Library

Library of Congress Cataloging in Publication Data
Scarre, Geoffrey.
    On courage / Geoffrey Scarre.
        p. cm. – (Thinking in action)
    Includes bibliographical references and index.
    1. Courage.   I. Title.
    BJ1533.C8S23 2010
    179'.6 – dc22
    2009045575

ISBN10: 0-415-47106-0 (hbk)
ISBN10: 0-415-47113-3 (pbk)
ISBN10: 0-203-85198-6 (ebk)

ISBN13: 978-0-415-47106-0 (hbk)
ISBN13: 978-0-415-47113-8 (pbk)
ISBN13: 978-0-203-85198-2 (ebk)

Contents

Acknowledgements   vii

Locating Courage   **One**   **1**

A virtue for all seasons   **1**

Courage as a virtue   **6**

Courage and reason   **11**

Rival paradigms of courage: Siegfried and John Wayne   **14**

Physical and moral courage   **21**

The Reality of Courage   **Two**   **30**

Courage, true and false   **30**

How to be courageous without knowing it   **35**

Courage and the explanation of action   **41**

Courage: will and spirit   **46**

Archbishop Cranmer   **56**

Cardinal Virtue or Macho Vice?   **Three**   **62**

"Mars is for men, Venus is for women"   **62**

Courage and patience   **68**

Why take risks?   **75**

Cardinal and special courage **79**

Fortitude Four 82

Courage and fortitude **82**
Fortitude and the self **86**
Patience revisited **93**
Should we be stoical? **97**
General Grant **103**

Courage and Goodness Five 107

Can we courageously do wrong? **107**
"Bad courage": for and against **112**
The intrinsic worthiness of courage **117**
Bauhn and Foot on "bad courage" **118**
Against the unity of the virtues **124**
Mercutio **128**

Courage: An Outdated Virtue? Six 135

Courage as a goal, and the goals of courage **135**
Modern courage **140**
Whistle-blowing **145**
Courage and the loss of meaning **149**
Doubt, certainty and tolerance **153**
Envoi **157**

Notes 159
Bibliography 167
Index 174

Acknowledgements

I am especially grateful to Alan Bowden, Tim Chappell, Roger Crisp, Michael Slote and an anonymous reader for the publisher for their incisive comments on an earlier draft of this work; their generous help enabled me to correct many faults (though no doubt many still remain). My thanks go also to my colleagues and students in the Philosophy Department at Durham for helpful discussions of issues addressed in this book and for their moral support (a useful injection of courage) in the writing process. A stimulating conference on the cardinal virtue of courage held at Viterbo University, La Crosse, Wisconsin in March 2008 enabled me to present an early version of Chapter Two and I am grateful to the organiser, Dr Richard Kyte, for his kind invitation to participate. It has been a pleasure to deal with the ever-helpful editorial staff at Routledge and James Thomas has been an exemplary copy-editor.

Geoffrey Scarre,
Durham,
February 2010.

One

A VIRTUE FOR ALL SEASONS

One night in February 1943, three students of the University of Munich painted the slogans "Freedom!" and "Down with Hitler!" on the walls of the city's most sacred Nazi shrine, the Feldherrnhalle, scene of Hitler's failed putsch of 1923. Guarded day and night by an SS honour guard, the building incorporated a memorial plaque to the fallen Storm Troopers, which citizens were not allowed to pass without raising their arms in the Führer salute. To desecrate this hallowed site under the very noses of the SS was plainly an act calling for the most exceptional bravery. For this and other acts of protest against the Hitler regime, including the printing and distribution of thousands of anti-Nazi leaflets, Hans Scholl, Alex Schmorell and Willi Graf, together with other members of the "White Rose" opposition group, were to pay with their lives before the year was out, many of them dying on the guillotine (Dumbach and Newborn 2006: 140).

Stories of outstanding courage such as that exhibited by the White Rose students can seem curiously inspiring and daunting at the same time: inspiring because they show to what heights of moral excellence human beings can rise, daunting because they provide a model of virtuous endeavour which many of us may feel to be utterly, and distressingly, beyond us. Courage, more than any other moral quality, tends to evoke feelings of admiration and awe, and courageous deeds are the stuff of legend and story (indeed, it has been calculated that bravery is the most prevalent theme in world fiction, surpassing even that of boy-meets-girl). Easier, perhaps, to esteem than to love, courage can appear to be an aristocrat among the virtues, the preserve of a rare breed of people possessing conspicuous natural nobility and greatness of soul. When we talk about brave deeds, it may seem appropriate to do so in a hushed whisper, while giving a metaphorical tug to our forelock.

Yet to portray courage as occupying so high a plane as to be beyond the reach of ordinary mortals is to travesty its nature and its role in the moral life. A wise and venerable tradition represents courage as being one of the *cardinal virtues* (along with prudence, temperance and justice), in other words principal virtues on which all other virtues turn (as a door turns on a *cardo*, Latin for "hinge"). According to this tradition, which has its roots in Greek thought and was widely accepted in the medieval period, the cardinal virtues are involved in all other virtues, so that we cannot have any of the latter without having some measure of the former. St Thomas Aquinas wrote in the thirteenth century that one "general characteristic" of virtue is the form of courage known as steadfastness – that is, the staying power that enables us to continue doing the virtuous thing even when the going gets tough (Aquinas 1966: 35 [2a.2ae.123, 11]). Someone who lacked the capacity to stand fast would not be reliably truthful, generous, loyal, tolerant, compassionate or forgiving; at the first whiff of difficulty or opposition, his virtuous efforts would falter. The cardinality of courage was recognised by no less a figure than Sir Winston Churchill, when he remarked that "Courage is the first of human qualities because it is the quality which guarantees all the others." We shall explore more fully later the sense and significance of the claim that courage is a cardinal virtue. For now we should note that if (as the appearances suggest) courage is bound up in other virtues, then it must be wrong to place it on a pedestal and suppose it to be the exclusive possession of a select band of brave souls – unless we very implausibly suppose that all human moral virtue is restricted to a very few. Courage, of some sort, must be at least as common as virtue is.

It would be a related mistake to suppose that all courageous action is heroic action. While many of our favourite paradigms and exemplars of courage are cases of almost unbelievable endurance or bravery in the face of danger, the virtue is as much at home in the cottage as in the castle, in the factory or office as on the battlefield. Our thinking about courage will get off on the wrong foot unless two things are recognised at the outset: that courage can be manifested in quite homely circumstances and that it is a quality that comes in degrees. It would have taken some courage for a citizen of Munich to attempt to pass the Feldherrnhalle without saluting, but not so much as that required by Hans, Willi and Alex in desecrating the Nazi holy of holies. Even the greatest writers on courage may have inadvertently given a misleading impression of the virtue by focusing on its manifestations in extreme conditions. Thus Aristotle said that the brave man is concerned with "terrible things," of which the greatest is death, while Aquinas proposed that the special province of *fortitudo* is that of "particularly serious dangers" (Aristotle 1954: 64 [1115a]; Aquinas 1966: 9 [2a.2ae.123, 2]). Yet these snapshot characterisations are needlessly restrictive. An office worker who stands up to a bullying boss, a person who dislikes heights but ascends a ladder to rescue a cat, or the nervous university lecturer who addresses an august conference in spite of her fears, requires genuine courage, albeit the dangers they face are relatively modest. Even the arachnophobe who steels himself to remove a large but harmless spider from the bath displays some praiseworthy pluck (though he may wryly recognise the foolishness of his own fears).

That courage comes in various forms and degrees was a fact acknowledged by that shrewd, if cynical, observer of mankind the Duke de la Rochefoucauld:

> Perfect valour, and perfect cowardice, are extremes which men seldom experience. The intermediate space is prodigious, and contains all the different species of courage, which are as various as men's faces and humours.
>
> (La Rochefoucauld 1786: 119)

La Rochefoucauld also noted that courage can be selective and intermittent: a person may be "brave at the sword, but fearful of bullets" or vice versa, and he may show more bravery on one occasion than another. If we should be careful to avoid (mis)representing courage by considering too limited a range of exemplars, we need to be cautious, too, about the inferences we draw from specific instances of courageous behaviour. To conclude on the basis of single cases of courageous or cowardly behaviour that someone is brave or a coward is undoubtedly too brisk, since — as our common idioms of "plucking up" or "summoning up" courage suggest — we can be more successful in finding the courage to do something difficult or daunting on some occasions than others. Moreover, since people have their own particular bugbears, they can exhibit surprising combinations of bravery and fearfulness (witness, for example, the reported cases of soldiers who will boldly face the enemy's fire but are deeply reluctant to visit the dentist).

Courage has always been one of the most prized virtues, and people who would unblushingly admit to their lack of many other qualities are commonly unwilling to be thought cowards. The gangster, thug or "hard man" who pays little respect to conventional morality and considers most of the virtues "prissy" would be deeply put out to find his bravery or boldness impugned. Praise of courage has been universal in all human societies, though there has been wide cultural variation in the ideals and expectations associated with it. Societies have taken different views on whether courage is an appropriate virtue for all or for some, for women or only for men, for plebeians as well as for nobles. While it has commonly been accepted that courage involves the mastery of fear, there has been less consensus on the forms that courage should take or the circumstances in which it should be exercised. Numerous paradigms of courage have been offered – the bold warrior, the religious martyr, the dauntless campaigner for social justice, the mother who raises a large family in conditions of deprivation – and each age must define for itself the kinds of courage it requires. Concepts of courage that are apposite in one social setting may be less so in another, or need adaptation or expansion; so many people today may regard as overly narrow the soldierly paradigm of courage which dominated the thinking of Plato and Aristotle.

Our English word "courage" derives originally from the Latin cor, meaning "heart" (compare the French coeur); and it may be no accident that the ancients took the heart to be the seat of the passions and of wisdom. In modern English usage the word "bravery" is a virtual synonym of "courage" and in this book I shall use the two terms interchangeably, though historically the former had a closer semantic link with the less obviously synonymous notions of daring and bravado.[1]

COURAGE AS A VIRTUE

In spite of the universal favour accorded it, the precise nature of courage is not very easy to pin down. Aristotle's influential account maintained that courage is the mean (*meson*) with regard to feelings of fear and confidence, describing as "rash" the person "who exceeds in confidence" and as "cowardly" he "who exceeds in fear and falls short in confidence" (Aristotle 1954: 40 [1107a–b]). Aristotelian courage is not to be confused with fearlessness but consists in feeling the appropriate amount of fear in any given dangerous situation and acting rationally in response to it. This may seem, at first sight, not dissimilar to the view of the contemporary psychologists Peterson and Seligman, who likewise refer to fear in their definition of courage as "the ability to do what needs to be done despite fear" (Peterson and Seligman 2004: 199). (Note, however, that these authors could more plausibly identify courage with a *disposition* rather than an *ability* to act in a certain way, since a person who was able but indisposed to face up to danger would be unlikely to be called "courageous"). But while both Aristotle and Peterson and Seligman think of courage in terms of a response to feelings of fear, there is a significant difference between the old and the modern authors. To understand what this is, we need to pause to examine a distinction that Aristotle and his followers draw between virtue and continence.

The basic contrast between the virtuous and the continent agent is that while the latter has bad appetites which he succeeds in controlling, the former lacks the same bad appetites. For Aristotle, both kinds of agent are admirable, but the virtuous is more admirable than the merely continent. Aristotelians hold that it is better not to feel attracted (e.g.) to steal goods from shops than to experience such attraction and resist it. A person who is tempted to steal something when the shopkeeper's back is turned has a weakness of character from which the truly virtuous character is free. Moreover, virtuous persons not only need not struggle against evil temptations but take positive pleasure in doing the right things because they are right. In Aristotle's view, while just, temperate or courageous *acts* can be performed by both virtuous and (merely) continent agents, justice, temperance and courage can properly be attributed only to the former. Because continence involves a struggle, it is also a less reliable basis for right action than virtue and sometimes fails, whereas virtuous people will regularly act well, as their actions "proceed from a firm and unchangeable character" (1954: 34 [1105a]). Therefore it is virtue, and not mere continence, that we should aspire to. We should aim to rise superior to temptation, rather than just to be good at withstanding it.

Aristotle's claim that just, temperate or courageous acts can be performed by continent persons as well as by those who properly possess the respective virtues raises the question of how we should describe someone who is disposed (in Peterson and Seligman's words) "to do what needs to be done despite fear." Does such a person possess the virtue of courage, or is he merely continent, mastering a fear which would otherwise prevent him taking the requisite action? Aristotle would say the latter. The (Aristotelian) courageous person is not a literally fearless person, but one who feels and acts upon appropriate fears in an appropriate manner, neither ignoring dangers as the rash character does, nor being carried away by his fears in the manner of the coward. He is a person "who faces and who fears the right things and from the right motive, in the right way and at the right time, and who feels confidence under the corresponding conditions" (1954: 65 [1115b]). Although in need of some unpacking, this formulation serves to position courage squarely within Aristotle's general account of moral virtue (*ethike arete*), which represents every virtue as striking a mean between excess and deficiency in regard to feelings and actions (on the ground that "both fear and confidence and appetite and anger and pity and in general pleasure and pain may be felt both too much and too little") (1954: 38 [1106b]).

As an example of true courage, Aristotle cites the soldier who "is fearless in face of a noble death" (1954: 64 [1115a]). This man has weighed up the pros and cons of staying put, made a rational decision on what is best to do, and cannot be deflected from that course by fear. Moved to act by his perception of the need to defend his country or his gods *and* of the nobility of laying down his life in such a cause, the fearfulness of his situation no longer counts as a factor to be weighed in the balance. He may perform his courageous acts alongside those of the merely continent soldier, who has simultaneously to fight an inner battle against his own fears, trying not to run away, but he alone is genuinely courageous, possessing the *virtue* of courage.

Influential though Aristotle's conception of virtue rightly is among contemporary moral philosophers, it would not be unreasonable to think his account of virtuous courage somewhat narrow and idealised. To hold that the soldier who successfully masters his fears and stands his ground against the enemy is not really *courageous* raises the question of what better epithet there is to describe him. Most contemporary speakers of English would feel little conceptual strain in ascribing a species of courage to him. Of course, modern Aristotelians might be persuaded to concede that there is such a thing as "continent courage" while refusing to call this the (or a) virtue of courage. Here we might want to ask, "What's in a word?" and think it a relatively unimportant terminological matter where precisely the boundaries of the term "virtue" (or Greek arete) are drawn. But the debate takes on a more substantial ethical dimension in view of the fact that, on the Aristotelian account, the "merely" continent soldier is significantly less meritorious than his strictly "courageous" counterpart – indeed, so much less so that he fails to merit the label "courageous" in any sense.

The chief objection to this view is that it is ungenerous, failing to acknowledge adequately the moral worth of the struggle that most human beings have to mount against their own myriad weaknesses of character. Departing from the strict Aristotelian line, we might prefer to see continence as a sort of virtue, and not the least honourable either. To this an Aristotelian might retort that it is better to have the kind of character that has no truck with vice, and that wholly fails to see its attractions, rather than to possess flaws which require to be overcome. But even if that be granted, it does not follow that there is not very considerable moral worth in resisting those temptations to vice that we do feel. What Kant called the crooked timber of humanity must devote much of its moral effort to keeping on the straight and narrow, as a more expansive conception of virtue might reasonably be expected to recognise. In this book I shall consequently talk about virtue, and about the virtue of courage, in a broader way than that sanctioned by Aristotle: one which, while acknowledging the distinction between (Aristotelian) virtue and continence, seeks to do greater justice to the latter by classing it, too, as a kind of virtue.

In fairness to Aristotle, there is one potential misunder-standing of his position that is worth forestalling. In praising virtue above continence, he may seem to ignore the fact that it is simply moral good luck that some people are born free of the character defects that others have to fight against. It is easy not to steal, or to stand one's ground in the face of danger, if one is born without the avaricious or the cowardly streak that may be another's downfall. One would scarcely deserve praise for having a fine moral character that was simply the gift of nature. Courage, like good looks or an aptitude for math-ematics, would be a desirable thing even if it were innate; but its possession would not then reflect any credit on the subject. But Aristotle firmly denies that nature equips us with the virtues:

> Neither by nature . . . nor contrary to nature do the virtues
> arise in us; rather we are adapted by nature to receive them,
> and are made perfect by habit.

> (1954: 28 [1103a])

Aristotelian virtue is not innate but acquired by habituation, in the same way that practical skills are: that is, men become "just by doing just acts, temperate by doing temperate acts, brave by doing brave acts" (1954: 29 [1103a–b]). If we want to become brave, we need to practise facing increasingly dangerous situations and trying not to run away. At the end of the process we should no longer feel any temptation to escape where reason tells us to stand firm. The virtue we acquire in this way is praiseworthy because it is the product of our own effort and not of nature's bounty.

It is intriguing to note that the process Aristotle outlines for achieving virtue appears crucially to involve the exercise of continence: the would-be virtuous agent embarks on a programme of progressively more demanding continent action until virtue is attained and further continence unnecessary. If virtue-seeking agents can be praised for the end they pursue, they also deserve credit for the hardness of the (perhaps lengthy) struggle they undergo. If continence, in Aristotle's view, is inferior to virtue, it is nevertheless crucial for the acquisition of virtue and deserves respect on that account; for without continence there would be no virtue.[2]

COURAGE AND REASON

One perennially disputed issue about courage concerns its relation to reason. For Aristotle, courageous action, like any other form of virtuous action, involves rational choice. The Aristotelian courageous man is someone who thinks before he acts. (I use the word "man" advisedly, for the Greek word for "courage" is *andreia*, also translated as "manliness," and Aristotle gives relatively little attention to the courage of women, which he evidently thinks at best a pale reflection of the male variety.)[3] As we have seen, in Aristotle's view all *ethike arete* "is concerned with passions and actions, and in these there is excess, defect, and the intermediate" (1954: 38 [1106b]). In order to determine the mean point relative to his individual circumstances, the agent needs to apply his practical reason (*phronesis*), which in the case of courage involves identifying the appropriate mean in regard to feelings of fear and confidence, avoiding both rashness and cowardice.

Yet the reliance of courage on reason has been questioned by some writers. As William Miller observes, it is often rashness that gets the job done – too much deliberation (as

Hamlet recognised to his cost) can paralyse action rather than procure results (Miller 2000: 157). Plato in his dialogue *Laches* noted that a soldier who chooses to remain at his post in the face of overwhelming odds may display "foolish endurance" yet still impress us more with his courage than another who occupies a better prepared and more sustainable position (Plato 1953a: 88–9 [193a–c]). People who perform brave acts often record that they acted on the spur of the moment, without stopping to weigh up the pros and cons. Soldiers on the battlefield sometimes display a spontaneous courage that seems as surprising to them afterwards, when they recall their behaviour in a cool hour, as it does to other people. It is not uncommon for combat soldiers after battle to look back at what they did as a kind of madness.[4] Thinking too much about what might go wrong can easily sap the will to act, even where the risks are accurately calculated and not exaggerated; such cautious attitudes better befit insurance agents than heroes. Pausing to ponder the risks can also lose us precious moments when instant action is vital: by the time we decide to jump into the river, the drowning child has been swept far downstream.

Nevertheless some kinds of risky behaviour seem patently absurd, such as playing Russian roulette with a loaded pistol for the sake of a bet or to while away a boring afternoon. Pointless risk-taking and acts of foolish bravado seem unworthy to be ranked as genuinely courageous, though in distinguishing the foolish and the worthy allowance should be made for cultural variations. What may appear to one society to be a vulgar act of showing-off may be regarded by another as an admirable demonstration of manhood. In a fascinating study of the Crow Indians of North America, Jonathan Lear describes the dangerous traditional practice of delivering a challenge by riding close to the enemy and touching him with a stick (known as a "coup stick"). While for the Crow this preliminary flourish to battle was a practice required by warrior virtue, to neighbouring tribes it may have looked like sheer exhibitionism (Lear 2006: 15–17). Most cultures distinguish between properly courageous acts and foolishly reckless ones but there has been considerable variation in where the line is drawn. Yet the common assumptions that there is a line to draw, and that courage ascriptions are sensitive to some standard of reasonableness, broadly support the Aristotelian claim that true courage involves a rational element. Rashness may sometimes get the job done, but there seems considerable cross-cultural consensus that courage should ideally be tempered by reason. Where "blind courage" in the absence of *phronesis* delivers the desired outcome, it will be more by good luck than good management. Perhaps the courageous acts which generally most impress are those that strike a mean between too much reflection and too little.

As well as inter-cultural variations in the demarcation of bravery and bravado, there can also be plenty of intra-cultural differences of opinion. Not all the members of the Munich White Rose approved of their comrades' daubing of slogans on the Felderrnhalle. One slightly older member of the group, Christoph Probst, roundly condemned it as a pointless escapade which put at risk the group's ability to pursue more effective modes of opposition (Dumbach and Newborn 2006: 140–1). Allow, for purposes of argument, that Probst's strictures were justified, and that the three students acted rashly. Does it follow from this that what they did was not authentically courageous? This is the evident implication of Aristotle's claim that courage and rashness are mutually exclusive (indeed, for Aristotle, rash deeds are a type of vicious deeds, deserving not even qualified praise). But many non-Aristotelians may feel strongly tempted to say that Willi, Hans and Alex were *both* courageous *and* rash. Denying their courage seems ungracious in view of their admirable intention of asserting civilised values and rousing a spirit of resistance to an appalling regime.

Miller has helpfully suggested that we should distinguish between rashness that is merely thrill-seeking or exhibitionist and that which is a matter of reckless means employed in the service of worthy ends (Miller 2000: 151). Following this suggestion, and classifying the White Rose action under the latter head, makes it possible to commend it as courageous without being committed to doing the same of playing Russian roulette or riding one's Harley-Davidson at a dangerous speed on the public highway. We shall have to return in Chapter 5 to the complex subject of the relationship between courage and moral ends (where, in fact, a note of dissent will be sounded with the claim that the ends of courageous action must be morally worthy, as distinct from displaying some practical rationality), but it is worth for now sounding a caveat about the Aristotelian hard line that forbids the commendation of action as courageous unless both the end pursued and the means involved measure up to high rational standards.

RIVAL PARADIGMS OF COURAGE: SIEGFRIED AND JOHN WAYNE

It is hard to imagine what it would be like to be frightened of nothing. For normal human beings, as for other higher animals, feeling fear is as natural as breathing. Most people fear many things, both great and small, and though (if we are lucky) we may never have to face up to our worst nightmares, few of us are unfamiliar with the sweaty palms and parched lips that are typical physical accompaniments to the emotion of fear. Fear is not, of course, a pleasant sensation,[5] and it often impedes our acting in the ways we think we ought. For those reasons, we might consider that humankind would have been better off if endowed with a literally fearless nature. But that would be a big mistake. For frail and vulnerable creatures like ourselves, a disposition to feel fear is a vital evolutionary acquisition, since it prompts us to take care of ourselves in situations of danger. Those who feared nothing would dare anything; and the consequences would all too often be disastrous. Fear, it is true, sometimes applies the brakes too sharply to our efforts; but it is better to possess brakes that are occasionally over-effective than to have no brakes at all.

A person may sometimes feel no fear in a situation that many others would find alarming. There are several possible explanations for this: it may be that she underestimates the extent of the danger, or that she believes herself, rightly or wrongly, to be invulnerable to the threats at hand, or that she is so world-weary or depressed that she has ceased to care what happens to her. A psychologically more interesting sort of fearlessness is that possessed by the person who recognises both the extent of the peril and her own vulnerability to it, is not indifferent to her own welfare, yet remains withal as calm and unmoved as if she were relaxing by her own fireside. If the fearlessness is real, however, and not just a simulation of sangfroid, there seems to be something decidedly odd about it. As the rational attitude to evils is to prefer their absence to their presence, there is nothing unreasonable about fearing such physical evils as death, wounds or injury (or, of course, for social animals like ourselves, such "social" ills as disgrace or disapproval). Someone who exhibited a generalised fearlessness in the face of danger or threatening situations might be suspected of some major cognitive and affective deficiencies, some incapacity for joined-up thinking or curious dissociation of intellect and emotion; and this suspicion has in fact been supported by recent empirical research. Studies conducted by Kochanska, Lykken and others indicate that a willingness to face situations that would cause normal people excessive stress is frequently associated with other components of the antisocial personality, including impulsiveness, a reduced ability to learn from experience, and a shortfall in such affective states as shame and empathy. Kochanska's work with young children has revealed a strong positive correlation between fearfulness and the development of pro-social attitudes. Children who are more disposed to take risks are less inclined to think about the effect of their actions on other people and are typically low on such moral emotions as remorse and guilt. They are also more likely to show "overall maladjustment and . . . callous and unemotional traits" (Saltaris 2002: 6).[6]

Just how odd a wholly fearless individual would be is apparent if we consider one of the most famous fictional examples of such a being, the young hero Siegfried, protagonist of the second half of Wagner's great opera cycle *The Ring of the Nibelung*. Siegfried, who has been raised from infancy in the depths of the forest by the dwarf Mime, has never felt fear and professes, to his own chagrin, not to know what it is. A strapping and boorish youth who fights fierce wild animals with his bare hands (when the opera *Siegfried* begins, he has just defeated and tied up a bear), Siegfried asks Mime to explain to him the nature of this elusive emotion. Mime proceeds to describe the "grisly horrors," the "terrible shudders" and trembling, and the throbbing of the bursting heart when one believes one is being stalked by a beast of prey in the dark; Siegfried, intrigued, replies that such curious sensations sound much to his liking: "Great is my longing for fear!" (Wagner 1960: 11–12). Mime proposes to teach his eager pupil what fear is by leading him to the lair of the man-hating dragon Fafner, a fearsome creature that stands guard over a huge pile of gold. Predictably, Siegfried confronts the dragon, kills it and removes the treasure, but remains as ignorant as he started about the nature of fear.[7] (Later, he also kills Mime, having learnt that the greedy, if also long-suffering, dwarf intends to murder him for the gold.)

Modern psychologists might see Siegfried as exemplifying the antisocial personality at its most extreme. But the important question for us is whether we should regard Wagner's hero as exemplifying one sort of courage or a lamentably unimaginative blockheadedness. Siegfried's insouciance in the face of danger is clearly quite different from the courage lauded by Aristotle, which, as we have seen, is neither fearlessness nor the mastery of fear, but the disposition to act according to reason while facing and fearing "the right things and from the right motive, in the right way and at the right time" (1954: 65 [1115b]). But is it any kind of courage at all? Can courage – of a sort – be ascribed to individuals who in threatening situations feel little or no fear, or are courage and (literal) fearlessness quite different things? But if characters like Siegfried are hard to understand, they are also hard to esteem. As Aristotle remarks, someone who feared absolutely nothing "would be a sort of madman or insensible person" (1954: 66 [1115b]). To have no fear where fear would be warranted is a species of irrationality, while there seems nothing commendable about facing a danger which leaves one emotionally unmoved. In practice we esteem much more highly those who master their fears and who, though shaking in their shoes, force themselves by an effort of will to stand their ground. Whether we want to call this "continence" or "virtue," it seems morally far superior to Siegfried-style fearlessness.

The actor John Wayne, star of countless cowboy films, proposed that "Courage is being scared to death – but saddling up anyway." US Civil War General William Tecumseh Sherman plainly thought the same. "All men naturally shrink from pain and danger," he noted, adding that an "insensibility to danger" was something that he had more often heard about than seen. Sherman's definition of "true courage" was "a perfect sensibility of the measure of danger, and a mental willingness to incur it" (Sherman 1990: 886). One attractive feature of the Wayne/Sherman view of courage is that it situates the virtue within the reach of ordinary men and women with a normal "sensibility to danger." If courage – or "true courage" – were the preserve of fearless heroes of the Siegfried stamp, then it would necessarily be as rare as they are. Courage on the John Wayne model is a virtue of the fearful, not the fearless, a quality that we can possess not in spite of the fact that many things frighten or daunt us, but because of it.

Does this imply that even a person with an excessively fearful nature – the sort of person we might describe as "fearing his own shadow" – could still qualify as courageous? No, according to Aristotle, since his fears are often unreasonable and untimely. But yes, on the Wayne/Sherman account, if he is sufficiently successful in mastering those fears. Courage is now perfectly compatible with timorousness, and, indeed, the more timorous a person is, the greater the scope (and practical need) for him to be courageous. Air Marshall Sir Timothy Garden has remarked that "One of the great difficulties of assessing courage is in measuring the degree of fear that each individual has overcome" (Garden 2001: 1). An individual's courage can easily go unnoticed by others who are unaware of her fears, particularly when those fears are idiosyncratic or unusual. A patient with Asperger's Syndrome may be fearful to touch surfaces of certain colours, a fear that appears utterly groundless to normal people. But an Asperger's sufferer who forces himself to overcome his inhibition against touching the disliked colour might nevertheless be said to exercise courage. (Courage of this sort, which involves mastering neurotic inhibitions and phobias, has been termed by Daniel Putman "psychological courage" [in Putman 1997].)

We sometimes describe as "fearless" someone who has "shown guts" when in a tight spot,[8] but usually we mean not that the subject was literally fearless but that she acted *as if* she were, forbidding her fears to hold her back from doing what she judged she ought. Strictly speaking, in such cases it is not the fear that is absent but its effects. We also talk in some cases about people "suppressing their fears," though this idiom is rather ambiguous between the distinct ideas of eliminating fear and controlling it. If mastering one's fears can be difficult, ridding oneself of them entirely is harder still and not achievable by a simple act of will. One cannot simply decide that one will no longer fear heights or small spaces or large spiders. To rid oneself of a fear, one has to proceed indirectly, say by undergoing a course of training, therapy or hypnosis; and even then one may not succeed. In any case, it would be unreasonable to try to eliminate reasonable fears, though we may need to be able to master them.

When Siegfried battled with the mighty Fafner, he was literally fearless and not just fearless in the colloquial sense of acting *as* if he felt no fear. But precisely for that reason we might be reluctant to say that Siegfried was brave when he fought the dragon. To merit praise for courage, it seems not enough to face danger unfazed; one must also take that danger seriously and care about the way that things will turn out. Tales abound of soldiers on the battlefield who have laughed and joked while shells or cannonballs have whizzed about them. Such nonchalant demeanour is a popular hallmark of courage. But if the indifference to death and injury is anything more than a gallant pose, then the soldier's courage is open to question: someone who genuinely doesn't care whether he lives or dies has no use for courage, as there is nothing he is concerned about losing. There is no need, in Shakespearean phrase, to "screw one's courage to the sticking place" if one has no preference for one outcome over another.

If it wasn't courage that Siegfried showed when tackling bears and dragons, then what quality was it? Plato and Aristotle would probably have labelled it spirit or spiritedness (*thumos* in Greek). Spiritedness is generally admired as a character trait, though it can serve bad ends as well as good; but a spirited individual at least has a greater potential to get things done and achieve results than one who is poor-spirited or pusillanimous. Spirit should not be confused with courage, nor does spirit of the "Up boys and at 'em!" variety have a firm claim to be regarded as a necessary component of courage (it does not seem to be involved, for instance, in all cases of fortitude). While *thumos* may have its attractions, it is dubiously commendable when found in combination with a reckless disregard of risk. Even a superhero of Siegfried's stamp, though he laughs at the dangers that worry ordinary folk, is not invulnerable and has objective reason to take more care of himself (indeed, in the opera *Götterdämmerung* Siegfried dies after being stabbed in the back by the treacherous Hagen).

Possibly the kindest diagnosis of Siegfried's condition is that he lacked the imagination to envisage what it meant to be hurt or killed. Not only did his nonchalant approach to danger expose him to excessive risks (as Mime sensibly asked, "What good is the trustiest sword, if you are lacking in fear?") (Wagner 1960: 11). Siegfried's deeper misfortune lay in his inability to feel the sort of fears that are the logical and psychological concomitant of appropriate self-concern. Courage belongs only to those who believe they have something to lose, and care about losing it. Someone who is without fear in a dangerous situation, not merely exhibiting but feeling indifference to the perils that threaten, is deficient in that concern for self that can plausibly be accounted among the basic features of personhood. Alternatively, if he insists that he feels self-concern but not fear, he demonstrates profound confusion. For a person who is (i) without fear where he (ii) recognises a danger to himself and (iii) has at least some minimal care for his own welfare patently exhibits practical irrationality; at one and the same time he both cares and doesn't care for himself.

PHYSICAL AND MORAL COURAGE

The first use of the expression "moral courage" recorded by the *Oxford English Dictionary* dates back no further than 1822. Forty years later, moral courage was defined by James Fitzjames Stephen as "readiness to expose oneself to suffering or inconvenience which does not affect the body," where this arises from a "firmness of moral principle" that is "independent of the physical constitution" (quoted in Mackenzie 1962: 12). Improving on this somewhat hazy characterisation, Henry Sidgwick in *The Methods of Ethics* affirmed that people show moral courage in "facing the pains and dangers of social disapproval in the performance of what they believe to be their duty" (Sidgwick 1907: 333n3). William Miller has suggested that moral courage came into its own in the nineteenth century when physical punishments of death, torture or durance vile for various kinds of protest, dissent and nonconformity largely gave way to the "softer" penalties of social shame or disgrace (Miller 2000: 263–4). So while the uncompromising sixteenth-century religious dissentient might have required the physical courage to face the threat of the axe or the stake, his Victorian counterpart would have needed instead the moral courage to cope with public vilification, dislike and ostracism.

It cannot, though, be true that moral courage has a place only in an age of civility. Earlier religious nonconformists faced the same range of social sanctions as their later equivalents, alongside the physical ones (though the threat of being disliked by one's neighbours must have paled into insignificance when compared with that of being burned alive by them). Man, as a social animal, has always cared about what others think of him, and it undoubtedly takes courage to imperil one's social position or to court public disfavour by standing up for unpopular beliefs or values, refusing allegiance to bad institutions, or protesting against injustice. Admittedly, one may have no desire to be respected by others for doing what one believes to be wrong; but one may still regret that one lacks their respect for doing what one takes to be right. Generally speaking, the more solitary the moral stance one takes, the more courage one needs to sustain it.

Ploughing a lonely furrow is inevitably more difficult than ploughing as a member of a team, even if the team should itself be a small and isolated group in the population at large. There can be no comforting *esprit de corps* when the *corps* contains only oneself.

At the beginning of his *Profiles in Courage* (1955), US President-to-be John F. Kennedy approvingly quoted Ernest Hemingway's definition of courage as "Grace under pressure" (Kennedy 1964: 1).[9] To commemorate the assassinated president and the high value that he placed on courage, and particularly moral courage, the John F. Kennedy Library Foundation of Boston offers an annual Profile in Courage Award "to individuals (often elected officials) who, by acting in accord with their conscience, risked their careers or lives by pursuing a larger vision of the national, state or local interest in opposition to popular opinion or pressure from constituents or other local interests" (Kennedy 2008).

In 2006 the recipient of the Profile in Courage award was the lawyer Alberto J. Mora, who, as the former General Counsel to the US Navy, had spoken up on numerous occasions against the physical abuse and degrading treatment meted out to prisoners held by the USA at its Guantánamo Bay naval base in Cuba. In a statement made in June 2008 to the Senate Committee on Armed Services Hearing on the Treatment of Detainees in US Custody, Mora recorded his invincible opposition to the use of cruel punishment or treatment that grossly infringed the inalienable moral rights of human beings, besides being strictly forbidden by the US Constitution. "If we can apply the policy of cruelty to detainees," said Mora crisply, "it is only because our Founders were wrong about the scope of inalienable rights" (Mora 2008).

While serving as General Counsel between 2001 and 2006, Mora fought persistently against the Bush administration's devious attempts to circumvent the law and facilitate the use of interrogation techniques at Guantánamo which, on any reasonable construal of that term, amounted to torture. Placing at risk his own career and promotion prospects, Mora began by taking issue with the legal advice offered by Senior Judge Advocate Diane Beaver, and accepted by Defense Secretary Donald Rumsfeld, that "extraordinary interrogation techniques" could lawfully be used on detainees; later, he strenuously opposed the so-called "Torture Memo" (which provided similar advice in more evasive terms) written by the Office of Legal Counsel deputy director, John Yoo. In accepting the Profile in Courage Award, Mora modestly protested that it was "too generous" to use the word "courageous" of his actions; this was a word more appropriately applied to the physically dangerous actions of US Forces personnel fighting on Middle East battlefields. Yet Mora conceded that physical courage was not the only type there was, and that the defence of human dignity and constitutional principles called on contemporary Americans to stand up against more than simply physical dangers (Mora 2006). There are different ways of showing grace under pressure, and Mora's was assuredly one of them.

The attention that many recent writers have paid to moral courage has produced a welcome broadening of perspectives, which were formerly too narrowly focused on physical courage, and especially the bravery of men in battle. While courage is undoubtedly a soldier's virtue, it is not exclusively a soldierly virtue. People called upon to defend their principles may have to lay on the line other things besides their lives. At the same time, to talk, as some authors do, as if physical and moral courage were two quite distinct genres of the virtue is to oversimplify a more complicated reality.

To start with, harms and dangers do not divide neatly into two clearly demarcated kinds, of which one calls for physical and the other for moral courage. Consider the following three penalties for making a public speech attacking some aspect of government policy: (a) corporal punishment of a hundred lashes; (b) official denunciation in the media; (c) loss of one's highly paid job, followed by a sharp reduction in one's standard of living. If risking (a) or (b) demands, respectively, physical or moral courage, what does risking (c) require? Having to give up goods that one previously enjoyed, e.g. being forced to substitute cheap plonk for expensive vintage wines, will be irksome; but will it generally count (in Stephen's phrase) as "suffering or inconvenience which does not affect the body"? Foregoing Château Lafite is not a violent physical penalty like being whipped in the public square, and saying that one needs physical courage to do something that may have this among its predictable consequences can seem strained; yet it does for all that have a physical element and is not obviously assignable to the category of "pains and dangers of social disapproval."

However, if that category is construed too narrowly, then moral courage inevitably sheds much of its importance. To understand "the pains and dangers of social disapproval" as meaning only those constituted by social disapproval, excluding all the further disadvantages resulting from social disapproval, implicitly trivialises moral courage. Mere bad-mouthing by people whose views one rejects may by itself be tolerable; indeed, one may even relish the accompanying publicity for one's own principled stand. In practice, individuals like Alberto Mora who have been praised for moral courage have normally had a great deal more than verbal censure or abuse to put up with. Even if they have not had to confront the prospect of death or physical violence, they have faced a daunting web of harms and discomforts involving physical, emotional and practical elements.

So we might think to preserve a distinction between physical and moral courage which avoids trivialising the latter by understanding the class of "pains and dangers of social disapproval" to include not only the relatively superficial harms of cold-shouldering and verbal criticism, but also the more serious evils of (e.g.) damaged career prospects, frustrated ambitions, loss of rank and influence, financial insecurity for oneself and one's family, exclusion from valued peer groups, and (at the worst) social ostracism. Even so, there remains something artificial about this move. Many of the evils which call on our courage are an inextricable blend of physical and mental elements, and it distorts the phenomenological reality to suppose that in facing them we bring two complementary kinds of courage to bear.

Think, for instance, of the punishment meted out to political prisoners in the former Soviet Union of imprisonment with hard labour in the Siberian Gulag. Being forced to work for very long hours in sub-zero temperatures, with harsh discipline, inadequate accommodation, poor food and rudimentary medical facilities, was clearly physical punishment of the most extreme kind. Yet exile to the painful world of the Gulag had also the symbolic meaning of rejection by the workers' state, the ultimate expression of social disapproval, and was keenly felt by many prisoners as such. Here the physical and "moral" elements of the punishment formed, and were meant to form, an organic whole: the harder the physical suffering imposed, the more emphatic the message of rejection conveyed. Imprisonment in the Gulag was an assault on both body and soul; it marked the individual as a bad comrade and citizen in part by scarring the physical frame. We can say, if we will, that prisoners who stood up to conditions in the Gulag possessed a courage that was both physical and moral. But this is something of a theoretician's analysis. Most of the prisoners in the Gulag probably saw their courage as being more unitary than that, an all-purpose grace under pressure.

There is little harm, however, in continuing to talk about physical and moral courage, provided we treat it as a handy *façon de parler* and not as signifying some psychologically deep distinction of modes of courage. It is useful in reminding us that courage has a wide range of objects and that courageous people are concerned with more than death, wounds and other solely physical afflictions. Commonly people who display one "form" of courage display the other too. This is not very surprising, for to take a firm stand against "moral" threats while being prepared to give way to physical ones (or vice versa) would suggest a degree of ambivalence towards whatever it was one was defending. If a cause is valuable, it is worth standing up for regardless of the kind of costs its defence may incur (though not necessarily, of course, at all costs). A seriously-committed person will do her best to withstand all threats, even if she finds certain sorts more daunting than others.

This has been a chapter of preliminary orientation, in which we have surveyed some of the forms and contexts of courage, looked at Aristotle's account of courage and other virtues, examined the role of reason in courageous behaviour and the relationship between courage and fear, and appraised the popular distinction between physical and moral versions of the virtue. More needs to be said on all these issues, and we shall pick up on them again in subsequent chapters. There are also many further questions about courage that we shall be looking at. For instance: are there any specific emotions necessarily or typically associated with courage? How does courage differ from other conditions to which it appears related, such as heroism, valour, daring, boldness, firmness, patience, constancy, perseverance, gallantry, "grit"? What is fortitude, and when and why is it praiseworthy? Does courage admit of distinctions on gender lines, with some forms of courageous behaviour being more appropriate to the members of one sex than the other? Has manly courage, as some feminist critics allege, been overrated in the past, consequently encouraging aggressive and confrontational behaviour where compromise and cooperation would have been preferable? Is courage always virtuous or can it serve bad ends (might there be, for example, a genuinely brave burglar or terrorist)? Is courage as important a virtue today as it ever was, or is there now something tired or passé about it?

These questions, and others, will be our concern in the remainder of this book. Not all will prove easy to answer, and the answers given to some will be controversial. But that in itself is testimony that there is life in the old virtue yet. Were courage wholly uncontentious, existing in the quiet hinterland of our moral consciousness rather than in the contested foreground, it would be, at best, a very boring virtue, one that had ceased to engage our ethical imagination. That concepts of courage can still raise argument (and hackles) shows how large a role it still plays in the moral life.

However, before we move on to other questions, there is some further preliminary business to attend to. The present chapter has outlined some of the salient features of courage and courageous behaviour but it has not penetrated very far into the philosophical psychology of courage. Since it will help considerably in tackling the normative issues to determine with greater precision just what courage is and isn't, this will be our main task in the second chapter.

Two

COURAGE, TRUE AND FALSE

"Brave one-year-old undergoes successful heart-transplant operation" ran a banner headline in my local newspaper some months ago. Such spurious and unrealistic ascriptions of courage as this may well cause us to raise an eyebrow. Attributing courage to an infant that had no idea of what was happening, and certainly did not choose to risk a dangerous operation, is an evidently absurd use of virtue language. But if we easily detect the well-meaning emotional manipulation that is being practised on us here, it is not always so simple to tell apart true cases of courage from counterfeits. It is not just that courage, like other virtues, can be falsely laid claim to, as it is, for example, by the traditional comic figure of the braggart soldier. The subtler difficulty lies in telling apart cases of genuine courage from others which resemble it – in T. S. Eliot's phrase, "flourish in the same hedgerow" – but are really instances of other conditions.

Consider this typically mordant passage from the Duke de la Rochefoucauld:

> The love of glory, the fear of shame, the design of making a fortune, the desire of rendering life easy and agreeable, and the humour of pulling down other people, are often the causes of that valour [*valeur*] so celebrated among men.
>
> (La Rochefoucauld 1786: 119)

This is La Rochefoucauld in characteristic form, deftly punc-turing our pretensions to virtue. True, he does not assert that *all* instances of courage are prompted by such selfish or shabby motives as the ones he lists. But should we talk about courage (*valeur*) at all where the underlying motives are dis-graceful? If I take considerable personal risks to bring down a rival, is it genuine courage I display? Aristotle thought of virtue as a state of character which takes pleasure in choosing the noble for the sake of the noble (*to kalon*) (Aristotle 1954: 36 [1105b]; 1954: 32–3 [1104b–1105a]). Thus on this view, a person who performs a bold deed with the ignoble aim of destroying a rival, or even the ethically neutral one of making a fortune, is not genuinely courageous, for his action lacks the necessary direction on excellence.

Of course, there is *something* in common psychologically between the person who acts boldly in a good cause and another who does similarly in a bad: both show a certain spirit and a willingness to take risks, and neither can be said to be a coward. But when we call someone "courageous" we are not merely supplying psychological information, as we would be if we described that person as having no fear of heights or as being terrified of spiders. For "courage" is not a purely descriptive term but one conveying a positive ethical appraisal. To be ascribed courage is to be ascribed a praise-worthy personal quality. The element of commendation that is intrinsic to the meaning of the term differentiates it from the term "bold," which in most people's usage carries no similar moral charge. So we can talk about an agent's deplor-able boldness but it would sound odd to say that someone showed deplorable courage (though this might not rule out that the cause in which he showed it was deplorable). The question arises whether it can be strictly *courage* that people display when they act boldly in a *bad* cause; for the notion of a virtue being deployed in the service of a bad end conveys an unmistakable whiff of paradox. But we shall postpone further discussion of this issue to Chapter 5.

Conceptions of courage vary according to how high the ethical threshold is set for the motivations which underlie the bold behaviour, and what kinds of motivation are allowed to count. In modern philosophical jargon, they differ in degree of moral "thickness." For Aristotle, no bold or spirited act exemplified the virtue of courage unless it was done for the sake of the noble and with an eye to enhancing the agent's personal excellence.[1] This is an especially "thick" and demanding notion of courage, arguably impracticably high-minded; it is implicitly very restrictive of which persons will qualify as courageous. La Rochefoucauld set the bar much lower. Courage (*valeur*) could still be the genuine article, and so worthy of some praise, even where its manifestations were tarnished by association with sordid motives. La Rochefoucauld seems to have thought of courage as a disposition to get things done despite difficulties, a meritorious quality of character but only contingently connected with any aspiration to the noble.

Recall Aristotle's brisk definition: "The man . . . who faces and who fears the right things and from the right motive, in the right way and at the right time, and who feels confidence under the corresponding conditions, is brave" (Aristotle 1954: 65 [1115b]). But now the question is, what are the *right* things, motives, ways and times to which the formula refers? In adding flesh to the bones of his definition, Aristotle proceeds mainly by a negative method, listing a number of circumstances in which we might be tempted to ascribe courage but where the right conditions are not properly met. By saying what courage is *not*, he evidently thinks we arrive at a clearer idea of what it *is*. Five such confusing simulacra of courage are distinguished.

First, courage is often attributed to those (such as Athenian citizen soldiers) who do bold deeds under the compulsion of masters or leaders who would punish them if they disobeyed their orders. Because their primary motive is fear of the penalties for non-compliance, thinks Aristotle, these people should not be termed courageous – though he allows that there may be an alternative virtuous motive at work in the case of those who are also concerned to avoid dishonour. Second, courage is not correctly ascribed to agents whose experience and practical knowledge enables them to face without real risk situations that would be dangerous for other people. Aristotle gives the example of well-trained mercenaries who take on untrained amateur fighters: although they may appear to be acting bravely, they know they are in no genuine danger from their opponents. Third, individuals who act from passion or anger, "like wild beasts rushing at those who have wounded them," are not brave, because they act blindly, in the heat of the moment. (We shall see shortly, however, that there is a difference between acting in the heat of the moment and acting on the spur of the moment, and that those who do the latter, though they also may not weigh the cost, can still count as courageous.) In a similar boat, fourth, are those naturally optimistic or unimaginative people, and sots who become sanguine through drink, who take risks lightly but only because they underestimate the danger or overestimate their own invulnerability. (Note in this connection that imaginative people who envisage in all its gory horror what can go wrong for them face a greater temptation to cowardice than their duller peers.) Fifth, people who face dangerous situations in ignorance of the risks they are running cannot be said to be acting bravely, for they have no fear to overcome, even though fear would be warranted (1954: 67–71 [1116a–1117a]).

One could agree with Aristotle that courage can sometimes be mis-ascribed without accepting all his divisions between true courage and its simulacra. He is surely right that someone who strolls across the flowery mead unaware of its being a minefield is not really being brave, though he may seem so to an onlooker who assumes him to know what he's doing. He may be correct, too, that "brave" is a misleading description of the person who "sees red" and goes, fists flailing, for a much more powerful opponent whom he would never dream of tackling in a cooler moment; "spirited" might be a better adjective for such a person. More dubious is the claim that soldiers who are compelled by their officers to fight, and who face severe punishment for disobedience or desertion, are not genuinely courageous, "inasmuch as they do what they do not from shame but from fear, and to avoid not what is disgraceful but what is painful" (1954: 68 [1116a]). This seems rather grudging, and not just because many of the Athenian citizen soldiers he cites probably needed neither sticks nor carrots to persuade them to stand firm before the enemy, being moved by a sense of moral or civic duty, or a desire to prove their valour to themselves or others. For even soldiers who have none of these motivations, and who would gladly run away if they could, may be ascribed courage if they manage to keep their heads and do what is commanded of them without flinching. Placed as they are betwixt the devil and the deep blue sea, in a hapless predicament that is none of their choosing, they can still decide between resolution and dissolution. Plausibly, standing up firmly to the enemy in spite of one's fear manifests courage, irrespective of whether there are stiff penalties for retreating.

Problematic in a different way is Aristotle's assertion that no courage is involved where a person is well trained to meet a certain danger, and possesses the requisite skills to counter it effectively. This claim is credible enough in circumstances where prior training or preparation can render risks negligible. But Aristotle may be overestimating how often this is possible. Danger is typically associated with unpredictability, and this is certainly true of the perils encountered in combat situations. Aristotle's example of the professional mercenaries who combat an untrained enemy is a weak one, since even the most accomplished fighters do not always have things their own way; moreover, any experienced warrior knows that the complacent assumption of his own superiority is a sure recipe for disaster. Even when the men can be told from the boys, luck sometimes enables the boys to have the better of the argument. Proficiency in arms will rarely reduce the risks to zero and eliminate the need for courage.

HOW TO BE COURAGEOUS WITHOUT KNOWING IT

Aristotle's *via negativa* is intended to throw light on courage by identifying some of courage's counterfeits – states which superficially resemble it but are not the real thing. In the previous section, I suggested that some of Aristotle's denials of courage implied too restrictive an understanding of the concept. Yet when we look for unmistakable cases of courage, the search proves surprisingly hard – so much so, in fact, that we could be forgiven for wondering whether the quality really exists at all. Is it possible that there is nothing but imposture to the status of courage?

It is often noted that third-person ascriptions of courage ("Smith behaved bravely") are much more common than their first-person equivalents ("I behaved bravely"). Furthermore, third-person citations of an agent's courage are often strikingly out of step with the agent's first-person reports: "I didn't see myself as brave; I did what I did out of love/ a sense of duty/ commitment to my principles/ unwillingness to let those bad people get away with it." It is not clear that such disavowals of courage should invariably be put down to self-underestimation or the virtue of modesty. One writer on the psychology of courage, Warren Poland, remarks that "[w]hat looks heroic to an observer usually feels inevitable to the individual involved. Hearing oneself called courageous, a person frequently answers, 'That didn't take courage; I had no choice'." Poland suggests that this "shunning of praise" is "the essence of courage," and that it stems not from false modesty or bashfulness but from the invisibility of his own courage to the subject (Poland 2007: 3).

In many cases of seemingly brave action, thoughts of personal danger are relegated to the background by loving or altruistic impulses ("How could I not have jumped into the water to save my own/ my neighbour's child?"), loyalty or allegiance to principles, persons or institutions ("I just saw what had to be done, and did it"), or moral indignation ("I couldn't stand by and see those poor people being mistreated"). The decision to plunge into the fast-flowing river is taken on the spur of the moment, without considering the dangers or reflecting that attempting the rescue is the rational or the noble thing to do. The suppression or suspension of thoughts of danger may not be the product of will; worries about one's personal predicament may simply get swamped by more powerful thoughts and emotions. The cynic's view that, when the chips are down, every individual cares chiefly for himself has been refuted by experience times out of number. Individuals frequently put their lives or well-being on the line for the sake of the people or things they care about. But is it right to pay tribute to the courage of the self-sacrificing agent who seemingly pays no attention to her personal peril? Can courage be the quality in play where there is apparently no thought of fear? Note that such an agent does not fit, either, the Aristotelian description of the virtuously courageous person, who *fears* "the right things and from the right motive, in the right way and at the right time" (1954: 65 [1115b]). (The person of Aristotelian courage might also be expected to be fully conscious that the quality she exhibits is courage.) It may seem better to praise the agent here envisaged for her loving kindness or her altruism or her adherence to principle rather than for her courage. Indeed, her motivational state seems closer to the Siegfried paradigm of fearlessness than the John Wayne paradigm of courage. Instead of saddling up despite being scared to death, she saddles up oblivious to the danger.

However, there is a vital difference between such an agent and Siegfried. While Siegfried's fearlessness is constitutional, hers is more likely to be a temporary suspension of self-concern in the face of grave threats to things she values even above her own life or well-being. Such a person is not, like Siegfried, an insensible dolt with an element missing from her make-up. It is not that she lacks fears in the face of danger; rather, she is for the moment *distracted* from her natural fears by the emotional or ethical imperatives that more insistently engage her attention. If she doesn't need to master her fears, this is not because she has none to master but because they have already been taken care of without requiring a specific act of will. She is effectively blind to risk because other things fill her moral visual field, squeezing out images of danger. Because she has not had to struggle against fear, she may fail to recognise her own courage; but her disclaimer of that quality should not be regarded as authoritative. Where fear has been relegated to the motivational background without an active struggle, it can still be said that the agent has acted in spite of fear. For if the disposition to feel appropriate fear had not first been suppressed – rendered motivationally inert – then the danger-defying action would not have taken place.[2]

John Wayne-type courage, where the subject is fully conscious of her fears, is not the only sort there is. Moreover, it is arguably not even the highest type. A person who doesn't need to combat her fears before saddling up, because they have been spontaneously displaced by more urgent moral considerations, might be thought to display an especially impressive brand of courage. In so far as she can be said to face the right things and from the right motive, in the right way and at the right time, her courage has some affinities with the Aristotelian variety, though the resemblance diminishes when her disposition to act is the fruit of nature rather than deliberate habituation, and to the extent that she neglects to estimate the objective fearfulness of her situation.

Modifying the John Wayne paradigm in order to allow that such spontaneous, unconsidered acts as jumping into the water to rescue a drowning child can count as courageous, does, though, raise the question of whether just *any* mechanism of fear suppression is compatible with the ascription of courage. And to this, the answer is plainly no. Imagine that Jim undergoes a course of hypnosis intended to rid him of his acute fear of flying. After two months of treatment, he finds himself able to board an aeroplane without anxiety. Is Jim being courageous when he sets out happily on his holiday flight to Florida? No, because he no longer has any fears to be reckoned with, these having been artificially removed. The elimination or suppression of fear by hypnotism eradicates the need for courage; and the same might be said of other manipulative methods of fear control such as the use of drugs, shock therapy, or surgical lobotomy of the fear-awareness centres of the brain.

It is true that there is no struggle, either, when an agent performs a bold act on the basis of forceful moral emotions or principles that allow fear no look-in. "When I heard the child's screams," says the brave rescuer, "the thought of my own danger didn't cross my mind; I just knew I had to jump in." But it would be misleading in this case to say that there were no fears to be reckoned with; it is not that the agent's fears have been eliminated, or buried deep in the psychic depths, as they were in Jim's case, but that they have been temporarily displaced by other thoughts and feelings which have forced themselves to the forefront.

Although it is not necessary that a courageous person should always have to fight to control her fear, it is essential that the source of her actions should lie within her, in a sense that is hard to make precise but which excludes all such external aids as drugs, surgery or manipulative mind control (e.g. hypnosis or auto-suggestion). (Note here that so-called "liquid courage" induced by alcohol falls into the same category; it is not real courage since as soon as the effect of the drink wears off, the fear returns.) When an agent is moved to perform a bold or risky act by her concern for humanity, her sympathy for the suffering, or her allegiance to principle, her act is an expression of her own personality, moral values and distinctive outlook on the world. If what is outside provides the occasion to act, the motive power to act comes from within and, consciously or not, disables fear; she acts, in other words, *autonomously* (literally, as a law unto herself). So too, it might be said, does Jim when he undertakes to be hypnotised to overcome his fear of flying. But Jim's autonomous decision to be hypnotised is meant to render any further autonomous effort to confront his fear redundant; his aim is not to develop the courage to fly but to remove the need for that courage.

It is fundamental to any defensible concept of courage, I suggest, that courageous action is self-directed action, where the agent is a law unto himself. But autonomous control of action is not an all-or-nothing affair. A person's freedom of choice may be constrained by all manner of external pressures, threats or difficulties which limit his range of options and enforce his conformity to patterns of action he would not willingly have chosen. And where autonomy is trammelled, it can be hard to decide whether, or to what degree, an agent is being courageous. Autonomy can also be threatened from within, by psychic disturbances or neuroses which compromise the agent's rational capacities. This is why we are not always willing to allow that suicides are courageous; a person who takes his own life while in a state of deep depression is less likely to be praised for courage than the soldier who throws himself down on a hand grenade to save his comrades.

Note, incidentally, that there need be nothing wrong with controlling fear by external methods, where more autonomous methods have proved ineffectual. Jim's recourse to hypnosis to overcome his aerophobia may be eminently sensible if all else has failed. Even the resort to courage of the liquid variety may be warranted when some risky action has to be performed and the genuine article is in short supply; it is better to go to the rescue of one's endangered comrades with the help of a drink inside one than to leave them to their fate. Yet if no blame need attach in such cases, neither will much praise for courage.

COURAGE AND THE EXPLANATION OF ACTION

One important conclusion to emerge from the preceding section is that there can be many and various motives at work in behaviour that earns the title "courageous." The existence of this variety might, however, cause us to question the value of courage talk. When we portray courage as a distinctive ground of action and a quality worthy of praise and aspiration, are we imposing a specious unity on a set of phenomena that are really quite disparate? Lumping together a wide range of states, motives and reasons for action under a common label runs the risk of blurring their differences. Would it be better to abandon talk of courage to poets, patriots and moralists, and promote clear thinking by pointing up the diversity revealed in the empirical facts?

Amélie Rorty sounds similar alarm bells when she writes:

There seems to be no specific set of dispositions that enable a person to overcome natural fears or reluctances, to take risks on behalf of a perceived good. The attribution of courage neither describes nor explains the dispositions, skills, or traits that assure the performance of fearful, difficult, risk-filled actions.

(Rorty 1988: 302)

"Dangerous and fearful actions," she adds, "form a heterogeneous class, with distinctive problems of attention and competence" (1988: 303). Heterogeneous, too, are the emotions that can accompany courageous action: anger, hope, desperation, compassion, zest, enthusiasm, repulsion, pride and a host of others. But if courage is not a single disposition – or a clearly-bounded set of dispositions – capable of doing useful explanatory service, then it may seem merely confusing to adopt a discourse that implies a unity where none exists. In fact, Rorty does not draw the radical conclusion that the concept of courage should be discarded as too vague, ambiguous or muddled, and nor, I suggest, should we. She is happy to countenance "courage" as a portmanteau term that loosely encompasses a wide range of dispositions, attitudes and actions that are meritoriously displayed in situations when the chips are down. Yet it is crucial to keep in sight the multiform nature of courage. As Rorty remarks, "it is one thing to face Achilles in battle, another to defy Nero, or to publish a scientific treatise defying orthodoxy, or to set forth to explore the North Pole, or to undertake to raise a child with Down's syndrome" (1988: 304). To homogenise courage is to distort it.

Saying, therefore, that someone acted in a particular way *because* he was courageous is generally of limited explanatory value until we clarify the specific motivation(s) involved. When Susie jumps into the swollen river to rescue drowning Sam, simply describing her as "courageous" leaves all the interesting questions about her psychology unanswered. Indeed, the courage that a person shows when she engages with risk or difficulty is more often the *explanandum* than the *explanans*: what is it about her, we still want to know, which impelled her to act as she did? What constitutes her courage, enabling her to do the needful in face of obstacles and dangers? It should be stressed that the claim here is not that courage plays no causal role in the production of acts of certain kinds. The point is that merely referring to *courage*, without going into further detail about the different sorts of dispositions, attitudes, desires and drives that may be operative, usually cuts little explanatory ice by itself.

That revealing explanations of an agent's actions need to probe below the surface ascription of "courage" may be one reason why people who act bravely rarely cite their courage in accounting for their own behaviour. In the most thorough survey that has been conducted into the motives of people who helped, or refused to help, Jews in Nazi-occupied Europe, Samuel and Pearl Oliner found no subjects who explained their behaviour by their possession or lack of courage (Oliner and Oliner 1988).[3] References to courage are similarly sparse in Ervin Staub's classic study *Positive Social Behavior and Morality* (Staub 1978–9), which carries only three minor references to the quality in the course of its 750 pages. Both Staub and the Oliners distinguish three categories of motives which typically conduce to helping behaviour in difficult circumstances, though their classifications differ slightly. Staub believes that "positive behavior" can flow from, first, "a desire for self-gain," second, "adherence to values, beliefs, and norms that were internalized, adopted as one's own, and/or developed in the course of experience," and, third, "empathy, the vicarious experience of another person's emotion" (1978–9: Vol. 2, 11–12). The Oliners' trio omits the first of Staub's categories (though they acknowledge it *en passant*) but includes his second and third; to this they add a further category of "normocentric" motivation, which they characterise as "rooted . . . in a feeling of obligation to a social reference group with whom the actor identifies and whose explicit and implicit rules he feels obliged to obey" (Oliner and Oliner 1988: 188, 189).[4]

The flavour of the Oliners' categories can be given by some examples. As an instance of an "empathic orientation" they cite the case of a Polish woman who, meeting a distressed Jew (an escapee from Majdanek concentration camp) who was hiding in some bushes, felt her heart go out to him: "He was shivering, poor soul, and I was shivering too, with emotion." Here the helper's empathic response was called forth by the sight of another's acute suffering and helpless state; the Oliners describe the woman's action as "impulsive, an immediate reaction to the victim's condition" (1988: 190). Although she realised her own danger in assisting a Jewish camp escapee, she washed, fed and clothed the man, and gave him money to help him on his way.[5]

Some "normocentric" responses were activated when a rescuer was asked, or ordered, to help by a person or body whose authority she recognised. For example, a woman described as "very religious . . . the wife of a parish minister" hid Jews, even though she was afraid, at the request of senior members of her church (1988: 199–200). The Oliners also describe an "internalized normocentric orientation" which leads people to act as they believe that members of their group should do, even without specific instructions. As one helper of Jews explained, "It's not because I have an altruistic personality. It's because I am an obedient Christian. I know that is the reason why I did it. . . . The Lord wants you to do good work" (1988: 207). "Normocentric" motivations, according to the authors, differ from "principled" ones which involve the subject giving orders to herself rather than taking them from others. The relation of principled helpers to the victims they assist is "mediated by a set of overarching axioms, largely autonomously derived." People with a principled motivation "interpreted the persecution of Jews as a violation of moral precepts, and the main goal of their rescue behaviour was to reaffirm and act on their principles" (1988: 209). One French woman who organised protection for many Jewish families gave as her sole reason for helping the principle: "All men are equal and are born free and equal by right." Helpers of Jews tended to distinguish broadly between a principle of justice (the right of innocent people to be free of persecution) and one of care (the obligation to help the needy) (1988: 213).

One might quarrel with aspects of the Oliners' analysis. While they concede that motivations of more than one kind can be present in the same person (1988: 188), their sharp distinction of "normocentric" and "principled" motivations masks the way in which people's allegiance to groups is characteristically mediated by their approval of the moral stances taken by those groups; at the same time, groups do not relate to their members simply in the role of givers of instructions, but group beliefs, values and mores may profoundly affect the personal moral positions taken by their members (which may accordingly be less "autonomously derived" than the Oliners suppose). Philosophical opponents of "principle ethics" may also object to the undefended assumption that practical moral judgement always or usually consists in applying general principles or axioms to specific situations. Some doubts may be raised, too, about the Oliners' further presumption that empathic responses represent spontaneous natural impulses or gut feelings that are independent of, and uninformed by, a person's value concepts. Plausibly, our disposition to empathise exists in dynamic relationship with the sense we have of the value – or of what Robert Nozick terms the "moral pull" – of the sufferer we confront (Nozick 1981: 400–2, 451–73).

But these, in the present context, are details. The object of outlining the Oliners' researches at some length has been to show how a number of different things can be going on when people can be said to act with courage. The Oliners nowhere suggest that "courageous" is not a fitting epithet for the people who rescued Jews at great personal risk. Nor, presumably, would they want to claim that courage played no significant role in producing such behaviour. But neither they nor their subjects find any use for blunt ascriptions of courage, recognising, as we should too, that the virtue is — so to speak — in the detail.

COURAGE: WILL AND SPIRIT

While courage is not a single distinctive motivational quality, it would be wrong to think that calling someone "courageous" is no more than a mode of honorific talk, the verbal equivalent of pinning a medal on his chest. While the psychology of courage is complex and multiform, there is, as Rorty points out, unity in the variety, courage being manifested in situations of danger and difficulty where feelings of fear, despondency or lack of confidence would be natural.

Simply saying that someone has or lacks courage, however, rarely tells us all we want to know. Imagine that when Susie jumps without a second thought into the fast-flowing water to rescue Sam, Sarah (who is an equally proficient swimmer) runs up and down the riverbank, wringing her hands. What makes the difference between the two women? To say that Susie has the courage that Sarah lacks, or that Susie is braver than Sarah, is not very illuminating even if it is true. (It may also, of course, be false; perhaps Sarah has less fellow feeling than Susie has, or doesn't greatly like Sam and wouldn't care so much if he drowned.) An Aristotelian might suggest that

Sarah lacks the appropriate degree of confidence in her own ability to pull Sam from the water. Alternatively she may have paused too long to consider her options and finds herself overwhelmed by the awful prospect of her own drowning. Here her fears, whether realistic or the fruit of an overworking imagination, have proved unmanageable, even if she judges that she *ought* to try to rescue Sam. A variant on this explanation is that the developing emergency causes her to panic, temporarily depriving her of the power of agency.

Explanations such as these may seem to suggest that courageous people are precisely those who *lack* certain conditions which sap the will or the capacity to act.[6] They do what has to be done in alarming situations coolly and collectedly, without being distracted by fear. To be courageous might thus appear analogous to being healthy, where health is defined as the absence of disease or of other debilitating physical conditions. However, this conception of courage is misleading if taken to imply that courageous action is the norm, and timidity and cowardice abnormal. There would be nothing very exceptional, psychologically or morally, about courage if it were the "natural" human state, from which only "sick" souls depart. This deflationary view of courage is unsatisfactory because courage demands characterisation in positive and not merely negative terms: brave people have something special about them that timid or cowardly people are without. The task is to say what precisely it is that enables someone to do the needful in a perilous situation undeterred by a danger that would have daunted many others.

In the remainder of this section I shall outline two promising accounts of the "positive" factors that make up courage. Because courage is multiform, it may not be necessary to choose between these; each might plausibly be seen as illuminating certain types and instances of courageous behaviour. I shall label them respectively the "fixing the will" and the "acting with spirit" theories of courage.

To get a flavour of the "fixing the will" account, recall the conversation between the evil Lady Macbeth and her husband when the latter has an attack of cold feet at the prospect of murdering their house guest, King Duncan:

> *Macbeth*: If we should fail?
> *Lady Macbeth*: We fail!
> But screw your courage to the sticking place
> And we'll not fail.
>
> (Act 1, sc. 7, ll. 59–61)

Ignore here the fact that Macbeth and his wife are engaged upon a wicked enterprise and consider the latter's pithy injunction to her husband to "screw your courage to the sticking place." Courage, she evidently thinks, and Macbeth's faltering purpose attests, is not a quality that operates unbidden; it takes an effort of will to bring it into play. We have to screw our courage to the sticking place, rather than wait for courage to screw *us* to the sticking place. Lady Macbeth's understanding of the nature of courage is well borne out in ordinary experience: when we wish to do something difficult or dangerous, we are often conscious of the need for an effort to get ourselves moving; we have to *make* ourselves act, in spite of the obstacles. Admittedly, this is not always so: a spontaneous rescuer such as Susie or some of the Oliners' subjects may embrace danger without making any conscious effort of will; when the will is already pointed in a certain direction, it does not need to be "fixed" there. But often it has to be. Imagine that Sarah, after watching Susie vainly trying to rescue Sam, finally determines to act and dives in after her.

Were Lady Macbeth a bystander, she might describe Sarah as screwing her courage to the sticking place.

There remains some obscurity about this picture. Is the effort involved in this kind of courageous behaviour one that creates a quality, courage, which previously wasn't there? Or does it instead tap something that is already present in an underground reservoir, accessible only with difficulty? (Unhelpfully, the common phrase "summoning up one's courage" seems more supportive of the second alternative, "screwing up one's courage" of the first.) However, both these alternatives can be sidestepped, and negotiation of the shady boundary between literal and metaphorical mind talk avoided, by employing the discourse of practical reason. Instead of debating whether some quality is created or raised from the murky psychic depths, we can speak about *acting in the way that our reasons for acting endorse*. That such an effort is sometimes needed arises from the fact that other, self-interested reasons are in play which prompt one to avoid the risky or onerous act, and which need to be rendered inactive for action on the endorsed reasons to be possible.

This account of courage is indebted to J. David Velleman's discussion of agency in a well-known paper "What Happens When Someone Acts?" Velleman contends that an agent can sometimes make a weaker motive prevail over a stronger one by "throw[ing] his weight behind" the weaker one. On Velleman's view, this amounts to reinforcing the weaker motive by another motive, namely the motive of acting in the maximally rational way (i.e. in accordance with the best reasons); and a person sometimes intervenes among his motives in this way because he regards the best reason as associated with the weaker motive (Velleman 1992: 480). A rational person desires to act in accordance with reasons, and where there is a clash of reasons, in accordance with the best reasons; and the operation of this desire is constitutive of his agency. Velleman further explains that for this motive to operate is for "potential determinants of his behaviour to be critically reviewed, to be embraced or rejected, and to be consequently reinforced or suppressed" (1992: 479).

It is characteristic of actions in general that they take effort (sometimes a great deal of it); but some acts that we would perform are associated with personal risks and costs that make us, as rational beings, think twice about performing them. What, then, provides the motive power when agents find the going tough? Velleman's story runs as follows. Imagine that someone initially feels quite strongly motivated to do some good deed but still more strongly motivated not to do it, because of the personal danger it involves. It might be supposed that the deed will not be done, since stronger motives can normally be supposed to overpower weaker ones. But not always, thinks Velleman. For the agent can choose to "throw his weight behind the weaker of these motives that are vying to animate his behaviour" (1992: 480). Where he desires to act in accordance with reason, he will endorse the motive that provides the stronger reason for action, even if it is psychologically weaker than the competing motive. In effect, he fixes his will. Velleman explains: "The agent is moved to his action, not only by his original motive for it, but also by his desire to act on the original motive, because of its superior rational force." What enables him to perform the act in spite of his fear is his rational endorsement of the weaker motive; and Velleman adds that this is "functionally speaking, the agent's contribution to the causal order" (1992: 479).

Contrast with Velleman's intellectualist account of acting under difficulties the psychologically more elaborate analysis offered by St Thomas Aquinas in his *Summa Theologiae*, which is a prominent example of an "acting with spirit" account of courage. Aquinas notes that while we desire many things because they are "beneficial" to ourselves or others, we also have to be ready to resist a variety of "contrary and destructive forces" which hinder those desires and deter us from satisfying them (Aquinas 1970: 207–9 [1a.81, 2]). On Aquinas's view, the sensitive part of the soul is comprised of two separate appetitive powers: a "concupiscible" part which desires what is suitable (that is, what is either intrinsically or instrumentally good), and an "irascible" or "aggressive" part which is the "champion and defender of the concupiscible" and attacks "the obstacles to what the soul wants and the threats of what it shrinks from" (ibid.). We need not accept Aquinas's faculty division of the soul to grasp the force of the point he is making: acquiring the good is often painfully difficult, dangerous or injurious to ourselves, and if we are to act effectively in spite of such hindrances, we need the forceful properties of mind or character that make this possible. For St Thomas, these are the passions belonging to the "irascible faculty" – or, as it might be called in more classical idiom, the "spirited part of the soul" – which includes not just anger (*ira*) but also daring (*audacia*) and hope (Aquinas 1967: 21 [1a.2ae.23, 2]).

The main difference between Aquinas's and Velleman's accounts is that where the former invokes an "irascible passion," such as daring, to provide the oomph to get the agent moving in spite of his fears, the latter's explanation centres on the agent's desire to do the rational thing, coupled with his recognition that the dangerous thing is, all things considered, the most rational choice. Both views acknowledge that courage involves defeating the forces that impede action, but while for Aquinas this represents the triumph of daring, for Velleman it is rather the triumph of engaged reason.

Applied to the case of Macbeth, a "Vellemanesque" analysis would portray the regicide as endorsing what he considers his strongest reason for action, that in favour of killing Duncan, enabling it to trump the weaker reason for sparing the king that has the (powerful emotional) backing of the fear of failure. Alternatively, Macbeth could be conceived as summoning or focusing the necessary amount of spirit to accomplish his desire – in Aquinas's technical language, as bringing the irascible faculty to the assistance of the concupiscible. Which of these accounts we prefer may depend on our reading of Macbeth's character. If we think of him as a cold-blooded, calculating killer, a man of stunted emotional growth, as poorly endowed as his wife with the milk of human kindness, then we might favour a Vellemanesque view for its emphasis on the role of practical reason in generating action. On this analysis, Macbeth fixes his will by throwing his weight behind the rationally superior motive, thereby putting all competing motives out of play. If, on the other hand, we see him as a man driven by powerful and conflicting passions, consumed by ambition while tortured by the fear of failure and disgrace, we may want to ascribe to him an exercise of the "irascible faculty," which supplies by a kind of psychological chemistry the spirit needed to neutralise the psychic obstacles to the pursuit of his predominant desire. Roughly speaking, the difference is between Macbeth's forming and his finding the courage to act. Arguably the former account provides an apter rendering of the idea of "screwing one's courage to the sticking place." But it could be argued that a richer account of the motivation of an agent like Macbeth might combine elements of both analyses. For each of the stories leaves a potential explanatory gap.

In the case of Velleman's, the problem concerns its handling of the phenomenon known as the weakness of the will (often referred to by its Greek name *akrasia*). It frequently happens that a person (i) considers a certain course of action, though personally risky, to be the optimally rational one to take; (ii) genuinely desires to do the rational thing; yet (iii) still fails to conquer her fears sufficiently to take that course. Velleman need not, of course, deny this. He crucially insists that for a person to act on her rationally endorsed motives requires her to "throw her weight" behind them – in other words, to apply her will to ensure that those motives rather than others are the ones given practical effect. A person who fulfils conditions (i) through (iii) falls at this last fence: she lacks the strength of will to act on her reason's endorsement of the weaker motive, so that her fears for her own safety win the day. Because her will is weak on this occasion, she fails to act as she thinks she ought, and as she would like, to act.

Weakness of will is often a remediable condition. But in what way is it overcome? A Vellemanesque account of agency will naturally look for an explanation to a further employment of reason. Over time, a person whose will has failed may continue to reflect on the reasons for and against acting until she reaches the inescapable conclusion that, as a committed rational agent, she really has no option but to act. Where at first her rational endorsement of the case for action was tentative and reluctant, fear kept the brakes on; but once she is firmly convinced that not to act would be unreasonable, then she throws her weight behind the favouring reasons.

There is nothing impossible about this story, but it is very unlikely to describe what happens in every case of firming up the will. For it is quite implausible to suppose that every case of persisting *akrasia* can be ascribed to a deficit of reason. Sometimes a person can be perfectly convinced that a certain course is the right one but still be prevented from taking it by fear. And where reason initially fails to get her moving, it is far from sure that further applications of reason will do any better. However, there is another possibility which this account ignores: namely, that she finds within herself the spirit to overcome her fears – or, as Aquinas would put it, her "irascible faculty" supplies the motive power that is otherwise lacking. Where one passion – the passion of fear – has paralysed action, what may be needed is not more thinking but the production of an effective countervailing passion. Indeed, if the overcoming of akratic states relied exclusively on the use of practical reason, one might fairly suspect that weakness of the will would be a chronic condition of the human race.

Should we simply, then, opt for Aquinas's account in preference to Velleman's? Unfortunately, this too has a problem. I described as a kind of psychic chemistry the process whereby the irascible faculty is supposed to remove or neutralise the internal obstacles (such as fear) which impede the operation of the concupiscible faculty. But the agent herself has become curiously invisible in this story; things seem to be happening *to* her rather than being done or controlled *by* her. Aquinas comes dangerously close to treating the faculties as if they themselves were agents or subjects when he speaks of the concupiscible part "desiring" things, and the irascible part acting as its "champion." Although these locutions might be passed off as metaphors, their employment disguises the absence from this analysis of any determinate role for the person whose faculties they are.

Here Velleman's account comes back into its own because of the greater importance it places on the agent herself as the source of her acts. Where Aquinas leaves us wondering what, if anything, distinguishes the acquisition of courage from a purely physiological process like digestion, Velleman by emphasising the agent's contribution to the causal order puts centre stage the subject who experiences the inner conflict of motives and makes up her mind to resolve it. The agent who throws her weight behind a particular motive does what it takes to make that motive effective – even though, I have suggested, this will often take a lot more than a further exercise of thought. She may need to find the spirit sufficient to overcome her fears, to fight passion with passion where cool reason is ineffectual. Screwing her courage to the sticking place is not just a matter of thinking the right thoughts but acquiring the right feelings.

These "right feelings" may extend well beyond the experiencing of a certain daring (Aquinas's *audacia*) or generalised spiritedness (Greek *thumos*). They include, for example, the intense anger or indignation one might feel at seeing a weakling being persecuted by a bully, which fires one up to intervene in spite of one's own fear of receiving a beating. Also inspiriting are sympathy and fellow feeling, and, in a subtler way, the proper pride or self-respect which impels one to face dangers and take risks rather than "let oneself down" by unworthy evasions.

However, sometimes courage does not have to be screwed or summoned up, because it is already in place and ready for action; here the psychic chemistry does its work without the need for a specific effortful intervention by the agent. When

Susie jumps into the water after Sam she may not need to fix her will first; her courage (whether the fruit of nature or habituation) is sufficiently well established to operate without any further prompting. Some of the Oliners' subjects were so intensely moved by pity for the people they helped that their courage showed a similar spontaneous quality (which is not to say that they were not acutely aware of the dangers they were running). As we saw earlier when discussing the Aristotelian distinction between virtue and continence, such agents may not deserve as much credit for fixing their wills as others do for whom mustering courage is more of a struggle, but they may well deserve more for the settled excellence of their characters that enables them to perform acts that most people would shirk. Courage is not only heterogeneous in its forms and instances, but also in its grounds of praise.

ARCHBISHOP CRANMER

Lady Macbeth's injunction to her husband to screw his courage to the sticking place was intended to stiffen his resolve and strengthen his faltering will. As a tailpiece to this chapter, we shall look at a famous case of akratic backsliding which was followed, after a short interval, by an act of quite extraordinary courage.

Thomas Cranmer was born into a family of minor gentry in 1489 and educated at Jesus College, Cambridge, where he took holy orders and became a college fellow, noted for his intellectual energy and industry. In 1529, Cranmer supported the controversial intention of King Henry VIII to divorce his first wife, Katherine of Aragon (who had failed to produce a male heir), and his practical suggestions as to how the matter might be managed in the face of papal intransigence brought him quickly into royal favour. Thereafter his rise to prominence in church and state was rapid, though Cranmer seems to have been driven less by vaulting personal ambition than by a dutiful desire to serve his God and his King to the best of his ability. Accepting with some reluctance the Archbishopric of Canterbury in 1533, Cranmer carefully steered the English Church through its break with Rome and defended his royal master's claim to be its supreme head while attempting (not always successfully) to exercise a moderating influence on some of the King's more violent measures against religious dissidents. During the short reign of Henry's son, the boy-king Edward VI, Cranmer's theology took on a more radically Protestant tone, denying the real presence of Christ in the Eucharist and rejecting the Catholic cults of relics and images. Cranmer oversaw the creation of a new liturgy to succeed the Mass, now officially abolished, and the beautiful cadences of the two prayer books of Edward VI, which have remained at the core of Anglican worship until modern times, were largely his work.

After the triumph, the tragedy. In 1553 Edward's fiercely Catholic sister Mary ascended the English throne, committed to the overthrow of Protestantism and the restoration of the English Church to its Roman obedience. Cranmer, walking a dangerous tightrope, enjoined all Christian people to be loyal to the new Queen but continued to denounce the Mass. Predictably, he was soon sequestered from his archbishopric, but much worse was to follow. Mary, who as Katherine's daughter had never forgiven Cranmer for his assistance in the royal divorce, ordered his imprisonment at Oxford on an improbable charge of high treason. In January 1555, Parliament was pressured into restoring the old penalty of burning for heretics, and the persecution that disfigured Mary's reign commenced, with fifty Protestants being burned alive at the stake over the following six months. Cranmer, however, was not among these early victims; the royal government had other plans for him. The Queen, who by now had married the ultra-Catholic King Phillip II of Spain, hoped that Cranmer could be induced by specious offers of clemency to recant his opinions and thereby deliver a stunning blow to the morale of English Protestants. To further the process, the imprisoned ex-archbishop was compelled to receive pastoral visits from a variety of Catholic priests and preachers in an attempt to demonstrate to him the errors of his ways.

Committed reformer though he was, Cranmer was uncomfortably aware of the paradoxical nature of his own position, since his support for the royal supremacy over the church made it hard to justify defying the Queen even when she was perversely intent on returning that supremacy to the Pope. Cranmer's perplexity over this conundrum seems to have combined with his very natural fear of dying as a human torch (plus, perhaps, some genuine doubt as to whether his views were right when so many learned men denied them) to persuade him finally to bow to pressure and recant. In a series of six statements, Cranmer confessed his intellectual and moral faults, accusing himself of persecuting the true Church, causing the death of "many good men," and opening wide the window to "heresies of every sort." As the "most accursed of all whom earth has ever borne," he said, he had merited the heaviest divine and human punishments (Pollard 1906: 373–4).

The government, while delighted at his self-debasement, now made clear that for Cranmer there would be no reprieve, and ordered his execution by fire for the 21 March 1556. Prior to the burning, Cranmer was to attend a sermon in the Oxford University Church of St Mary, in which Dr Cole, the

Provost of Eton, would summarise his crimes and invite the former archbishop publicly to repudiate his heresies. But the Queen and her advisers had badly underestimated their man. A hushed audience in St Mary's listened while Dr Cole reminded Cranmer of his mistakes and urged the congregation to pray for the contrite sinner. Cranmer, who was seen to weep while Cole was speaking, then opened his own address with a prayer. What happened next was entirely unexpected. Departing without warning from the pre-agreed script, Cranmer forcefully repudiated not his Protestant beliefs but his former recantation of them "contrary to the truth I thought in my heart" (MacCulloch 1996: 603). The seventeenth-century historian Gilbert Burnet takes up the story:

> he in most pathetic expressions confessed his sin, that the hopes of life had made him sign a paper contrary to the truth, and against his conscience: and he had therefore resolved, that the hand that signed it, should be burnt first; he also declared that he had the same belief concerning the sacrament, which he had published in the book he writ about it. Upon this there was a great consternation in the assembly, but they resolved to make an end of him suddenly; so without suffering him to go further, they hurried him away to the stake, and gave him all the disturbance they could, by their reproaches and clamours: but he made them no answer, having now turned his thoughts wholly to God. When the fire was kindled, he held his right hand towards the flame, till it was consumed, and often said *that unworthy hand*; he was soon after quite burnt.

(Burnet 1684: 328)

This astonishing example of courageous action succeeding an episode of *akrasia* shows what is possible when a person screws his courage to the sticking place. To be sure, Cranmer's final defiant stand could be argued to be the act of a man who knew he has nothing more to lose. Yet the available evidence suggests that Cranmer was deeply ashamed of his submission to pressure, and his resolute holding of his hand in the flame is strong testimony to the sincerity of his repentance. Velleman might describe him as throwing his weight behind the motives which his reason (eventually) endorsed. He might also be characterised as finding the spirit to do what needed to be done. Perhaps both these descriptions correctly locate an aspect of the psychological reality. Cranmer himself made no claim to being a brave man, and is said to have told a friend that what natural audacity he possessed had been knocked out of him in childhood by a brutal schoolmaster. His biographer A. F. Pollard describes him as being of "that shrinking, sensitive nature which usually acts like a red rag on bullies," adding that he had "none of the hardihood which ignorance breeds, nor the courage which springs from an incapacity to realise danger and suffering." Nevertheless "when once his mind was made up his courage was not found lacking" (Pollard 1906: 328).

Cranmer's case also raises another point of general interest. Pollard describes him as lacking a courageous character but as able to muster courage "when once his mind was made up." The first part of this description adverts to the fact that Cranmer did not consistently act in a brave fashion, and that he was sometimes browbeaten into acting against his better judgement. It may thus seem tantamount to denying that Cranmer possessed the virtue (*arete*) of courage, where this is understood as a settled disposition of character, reliably manifested on suitable occasions.[7] Pollard might prefer to say that Cranmer displayed a virtuous courage episodically or intermittently, on those occasions when "his mind was made up." Yet this would still be to recognise in Cranmer a certain disposition, namely, the disposition to act in a bold and defiant manner when the chips were really down. While the Archbishop could be daunted by danger, there were limits beyond which he could not be pushed. The moral of this is that courage that is reserved for such special occasions is still courage, and can properly be regarded as part of the character of people whose watchword might be "Thus far but no further."

Three

> Then out spake brave Horatius,
> The captain of the Gate:
> To every man upon this earth
> Death cometh soon or late.
> And how can man die better
> Than facing fearful odds,
> For the ashes of his fathers,
> And the temples of his gods?
>
> Thomas Babington Macaulay,
> "Horatius: A Lay about the Year of
> the City CCCLX," stanza 27 (Macaulay 1897)

"MARS IS FOR MEN, VENUS IS FOR WOMEN"

Lord Macaulay's famous poem, once familiar to every British schoolchild, recounts how the ancient Roman hero Horatius, with two equally stalwart companions, held the narrow bridge across the River Tiber against a powerful Etruscan army. The saving of Rome by the "dauntless Three" exemplified not one but two prime virtues honoured in an imperialistic age (though not only then): manly courage and selfless devotion to one's country or community. It is truistic to remark that the combination of these can be the source of much good or much evil. Sometimes personal valour applied in a bad national cause has disastrous effects on life, liberty and property, but it can also serve to maintain the right, as when British soldiers and citizens displayed the celebrated "Dunkirk spirit" in the dangerous high summer of 1940, when menaced with invasion by a seemingly invincible Nazi Germany.

I write these words on 11 November 2008, the ninetieth anniversary of the end of the Great War – the so-called "war to end wars" that led only to war, the Second World War, which began a mere twenty-one years later. Today ceremonies are being held throughout Europe and in many parts of the world to remember the dead combatants of 1914–18, and to honour their courage and endurance in almost intolerable conditions. But paying respect to the memory of those who fought and died does not imply approving of the cause for which they were, as many now think, needlessly and culpably sacrificed by national leaders who blithely accepted Clausewitz's dictum that war is merely the continuation of politics by other means. What was that cause? The question, as historians are agreed, has no simple answer. Greed, fear, insecurity, envy, national pride, self-aggrandisement, and not least what the Italians called *sacro egoismo* were elements in the lethal mix; but helping to flavour and make it more palatable (in an age when almost all politicians were men) were old-fashioned concepts of masculine virtue, chivalrous hangovers from a former age which preferred death to dishonour. What the British war poet Wilfred Owen was to term "the old lie" *dulce et decorum est pro patria mori* (it is sweet and fitting to die for one's country) seemed an evident, innocent truth in the febrile days of 1914, when French cavalry rode into battle in gaily coloured uniforms to make a gallant impression on the enemy.

It is a sign of changed times that almost as much attention has been devoted by the British media in recent days to the courage of those who refused to fight in the Great War as to that of those who did. Once a despised or, at best, a marginalised class, the conscientious objectors of 1914–18 have become a type of modern hero to people who value moral courage alongside, or even before, physical courage. Doubtless not all those who professed conscientious scruples were sincere in their protestations; some may have laid claim to moral or religious reservations to cover more self-interested reasons for not fighting. Those who had little self-respect may have cared little about forfeiting the respect of others. Yet it must have taken a very firm act of will for genuine conscientious objectors to expose themselves to moral opprobrium when they sought to do the morally honourable thing. Acting, as Aristotle would have described them, for the sake of the noble, their reward was to be derided as ignoble cowards, unmanly men who left it to others to protect their homes and families and the temples of their gods.

Not all conscientious objectors rejected the very questionable gender stereotypes that underlay the condemnation of their refusal to fight as unmanly. Some simply saw no point in the slaughterhouse of the Western Front, where each tiny bit of ground was won from the enemy at the cost of innumerable human lives. But more fundamental questioning was also under way about traditional conceptions of masculinity and male virtue. When courage and the ideals normally associated with it (honour, loyalty, steadfastness, male protection of women and the weak) could produce something as terrible as the First World War, courage looked due for a reappraisal. If "by their fruits you shall know them" applies to virtues, then the claims of manly courage to be one had become dubious in an age when warfare had become an industrialised process for the mass-production of death.

Amélie Rorty has remarked that "Even when courage acts for something or moves to something, it is defined as persistence against what is conceived as a resisting opponent." A person who acts bravely perceives "the objects requiring courage . . . as external others, to be overcome or endured" (Rorty 1988: 300). This prompts the worry that courage is antithetical to compromise, conciliation and the search for peaceful solutions to problems. Courageous people may incline to fight when they should talk, and dig in their heels rather than see what can be accomplished by good will and diplomacy. They stand on their rights and make doing so a point of honour. Even worse, thinks Rorty, those who value the virtue may deliberately seek out opportunities to be courageous and read "situations in such a way as to elicit relevant actions and reactions" (1988: 300). Wanting to be seen as individuals who cannot be pushed around, their typical stance is a combative one even when conciliation would serve mutual interests better. Not for them La Rochefoucauld's prudential counsel that "A wise man had rather avoid an engagement than embrace a conquest" (La Rochefoucauld 1786: 122). They stick to their guns not just figuratively but often literally too.

The association of courage, so conceived, with a certain conception of masculinity is readily apparent. The Greek and Latin words for "courage," namely *andreia* and *virtus* respectively, point to this identification with the male sex even more forcefully, deriving as they do from the words for "man" (*andros* and *vir*).[1] Harvey Mansfield writes that "A manly man asserts himself so that he and the justice he demands are not overlooked" (Mansfield 2006: x). Men stick up bravely for themselves and for those to whom they owe protection. Those who fail or refuse to do so are judged not only cowardly but womanish, and are liable to be despised by men and women alike. (Interestingly in this connection, those who handed out white feathers to "cowardly" men during the Great War were generally women.) If the tutelary deity of the female sex is Venus, the goddess of love, that of the male is Mars, the redoubtable god of war.

The identification of courage as a quintessentially male virtue, and in particular the virtue of warriors on the battle-field, was made explicitly by Aristotle. Allowing that it took a quality resembling courage to face up to poverty and disease, Aristotle considered that courage, in the strictest sense of the term, belonged only to the man who stood his ground before what was most awe-inspiring, namely death – and even then, not death in just any circumstances but death in battle, which allowed the greatest scope to demonstrate nobility: "Properly, then, he will be called brave who is fearless in face of a noble death, and of all emergencies that involve death; and the emergencies of war are in the highest degree of this kind" (Aristotle 1954: 64 [1115a]). On this narrow view, even a traveller by sea who keeps his head when his ship is faced with imminent shipwreck is not really courageous, since death at sea lacks nobility and offers no opportunity to show prowess (1954: 64–5 [1115a–b]).[2]

Plato, in his dialogue *Laches*, offers a somewhat more expansive conception of courage, though he too draws his chief paradigms of the virtue from a male and military context. Still, it is refreshing to hear Socrates clarify in the following broader terms his request to the old general, Laches, to explain what courage is:

> For I meant to ask you not only about the courage of the heavy-armed soldiers, but about the courage of cavalry and every other style of soldier; and not only who are courageous in war, but who are courageous in perils by sea, and who in

disease, or poverty, or again in politics, are courageous; and
not only who are courageous against pain or fear, but mighty
to contend against desires and pleasures, either fixed in their
rank or turning upon the enemy.

(Plato 1953a: 86 [191c–e])

Strikingly in this passage, even non-military threats and difficulties that need to be faced with courage are pictured
as "enemies" arranged in "ranks," indicating how deeply
imbued with ideas of force and combat Plato's thinking about
courage was.

But alternative conceptions of the virtue are possible. In the
poem "Strange Meeting," Wilfred Owen's dead German soldier, in recounting what he has lost through death, includes
the opportunity to show moral courage and wisdom in bringing home to men "the truth untold, The pity of war, the
pity war distilled." By their ignorance of this, they cause civil-
isation to go backwards – the "nations trek from progress" –
and men either rest content with a spoiled, imperfect world
or "boil bloody," ready to kill one another with tigerish
swiftness. Had death not intervened –

Then, when much blood had clogged their chariot-wheels
I would go up and wash them from sweet wells,
Even with truths that lie too deep for taint.
I would have poured my spirit without stint
But not through wounds; not on the cess of war.

(Owen 1973: 102)

This is a very un-Aristotelian perspective. But perhaps even
to the "master of those who know" (as Dante characterised
Aristotle) some truths were opaque. At any rate, in the early
twenty-first century it seems no longer so far-fetched to

discover nobility in those who do not fight, but who attempt to restrain or discourage others from fighting. There may be many more facets to courage than Aristotle acknowledged.

COURAGE AND PATIENCE

The twentieth-century's experience of total war has not been the only source of challenges to traditional ideas of masculine virtue. Feminists (of both sexes) have likewise taken issue with conventional stereotypes of male and female nature and social role: stereotypes which have mostly represented women as inferior physically, mentally and morally to men. St Peter's opinion of woman as "the weaker vessel" has lingered on well into modern times (1 Pet. 3:7), and in certain places it does so still. Female virtues have generally been taken to be such less assertive ones as patience, gentleness, modesty, quietness and obedience to their male masters (husbands, fathers, brothers). With the exception of the last, these may seem, in abstraction, honourable virtues which anyone might be proud of; but in the context of actual women's lives their inculcation has tended to reinforce their subservience to men and block their access to positions of power, influence and independence. If women themselves are persuaded that man's place is in the forum and woman's in the home, then they are less likely, in Sabina Lovibond's words, "to learn to conceptualize their possible resentment of the conditions of their life" (Lovibond 1983: 199). Since too much self-assertion by women can make things difficult for men, it is far better (for men) if women cultivate the passive virtues of patience and quiet endurance. And they are more likely to do this if they believe that active courage is best left to the menfolk.

A vignette from Charles Dickens' novel *Oliver Twist* gives the taste of centuries-old attitudes. The butler and footman at a lonely country house have been alarmed one night at hearing the brutal burglar Bill Sikes attempting to break into the premises. Recounting the adventure afterwards, Mr Giles the butler puts a Falstaffian spin on the courage he was far from feeling at the time:

> "Brittles," I says, when I had woke him, "don't be frightened!
> . . . We're dead men, I think, Brittles," I says, continued Giles; "but don't be frightened."
>
> "*Was* he frightened?" asked the cook.
>
> "Not a bit of it," replied Mr Giles. "He was as firm – ah! pretty near as firm as I was."
>
> "I should have died at once, I'm sure, if it had been me," observed the housemaid.
>
> "You're a woman," retorted Brittles, plucking up a little.
>
> "Brittles is right," said Mr Giles, nodding his head approvingly; "from a woman, nothing else was to be expected."
>
> (Dickens 1985: 222)

Too wise himself to take such stereotypical ideas seriously, Dickens was happy to subject them to kindly ridicule. But for many generations of women they were no laughing matter. One much older literary text put men and women firmly in their respective places. Pericles' funeral speech over the Athenian dead of the Peloponnesian War, as related by Thucydides, commemorated the men who had died in glorious combat for their country.[3] According to Pericles, "a death such as theirs gives the true measure of a man's worth; it may be the first revelation of his virtues, but is at any rate their final seal." Even those who had never shone in their lives before had redeemed their reputation by their mode of leaving them: "they have blotted out the evil with the good, and have benefited the state more by their public services than they have injured her by their private actions." *Andreia* exerted in the service of the fatherland was more than enough to square the moral balance sheet, however great the previous deficit. None of this applied to women, though:

> [I]f I am to speak of womanly virtues to those of you who will henceforth be widows, let me sum them up in one short admonition: To a woman not to show more weakness than is natural to her sex is a great glory, and not to be talked about for good or for evil among men.
>
> (Thucydides 1994: 98,100 [Bk 2, paras 42, 46])

This is blatant damnation by faint praise. If the best that can be expected from a woman is that she should hide her native frailty, then the benchmark of virtue is plainly being set much lower for women than for men. True, women were known who had acted like men in defying danger for the sake of what they thought to be right. The story of Antigone, who was punished with death for burying the body of her dead brother against the orders of King Creon, would have been very familiar to Pericles and every Greek. But such women were unusual and highly disturbing in their assumption of a male role. When it came to glory, women were meant to bask only in that which they reflected from their menfolk. In Athenian ideology, as in many later ideologies including those of traditional Christianity and Islam, man is the sun and woman the moon, shining only at second-hand.

At this point the reader could be forgiven for wondering exactly what is supposed to be wrong with courage, and with its claim to be a virtue. For the critique so far seems to have proceeded in two rather different directions. First, the virtuous status of courage was questioned on the ground that those who cultivate it too often become combative, uncompromising, stubborn and hard. Pericles' praise of the Athenian dead for their services to the state was silent on the havoc they had wrought on other Greeks in the quest for hegemony and empire. And Pericles showed no awareness of the internal damage that a person may do to himself when he systematically prefers assertiveness to sensitivity, toughness to gentleness – not to mention the more overt harms he risks by his itchiness to defend his manly honour. On this perspective, courage seems less a virtue than a macho vice.

But second, the exclusion of women from the class of the fittingly courageous was criticised as a means of keeping women out of a man's world, making them feel naturally and morally inferior, and confining them to a limited sphere of action in which the pertinent virtues are of the second rank. The refusal to allow that women could, or should, be courageous in the masculine mode was seen as restricting women's ability to compete with men for the good things of life. Rather than emulate the bold and brash Sir Lancelot, they were supposed to model themselves on the Patient Griselda, in medieval story the archetype of the wholly uncomplaining, obedient wife.

Yet the question is why women should care about male attempts to convince them that courage is not for them if courage, as men conceive it, is actually a bogus virtue. If it is better to be tender rather than tough, and sensible instead of chivalrous; if wise people prefer conciliation to conflict, don't always stand on their rights or dignity, and avoid unnecessary risks or foolish self-sacrifice; then the kind of courage praised by Aristotle and Pericles sheds much of its attraction. The question is why women should wish to fall in with a male pattern of virtue when their own more typical virtues can credibly be regarded as superior. Might their frustration at being excluded from this pattern reflect their own regrettable indoctrination into a view of the world that has passed its sell-by date?

The response to this question involves rejecting the over-simplifications on which it rests. Women who rightly refuse to model themselves on Patient Griselda are mostly far from wanting to imitate Sir Lancelot. A lot of moral space lies in between these extremes of self-affirmation and self-negation, and this intermediate space has room for both sexes. To suppose that courage and patience are opposed ideals, or that courageous people cannot be patient or patient people courageous, is to misunderstand both virtues. As Eamonn Callan writes, there is no "deep and ineradicable tension" between patience and courage; indeed, "[t]here is no less reason to prize patience than there is to value courage, and no less reason to despise impatience than there is to loathe cowardice" (Callan 2005: 204). Courage is not essentially associated with brutality, pitilessness and violence, any more than patience inevitably goes along with a pusillanimous readiness to accept abuse without resentment. Most virtues have travestied or exaggerated forms in which they metamorphose into vices, and courage and patience are not unique in this. So overgenerosity may kill with kindness, unstinting candour can be cruelly unsparing of feelings, uncompromising loyalty to X can be productive of serious injustice to Y. Plausibly, what both sexes should aspire to are forms of courage and patience that are consonant with one another and with other virtues.

Beautifully demonstrating how courage and patience, far from necessarily excluding each other, can come together in dynamic partnership, is the career of the trade unionist and campaigner for women's rights, Mary Macarthur, a major figure in the British women's movement before her premature death from cancer in 1921. A living refutation of Periclean or Petrine views of the mental and moral feebleness of women, Macarthur combined the courage to pursue justice in the face of great odds with the patience to work steadily away at changing blinkered attitudes. Mary was the daughter of a deeply conservative Scottish draper who sent her, while still in her teens, to spy on the activities of the Ayr branch of the Shop Assistants' Union. But Mary was so moved by what she learned at their meetings about local employers' mistreatment of their workers that she became, to her father's dismay, an energetic trade-union organiser and socialist, dedicated especially to improving the lot of labouring women. By the turn of the twentieth century Mary was closely associated with the founders of the Independent Labour Party and had gained a reputation as a powerful speaker at political and trade union events. In 1903 she became Secretary of the Women's Trade Union League, and two years later started a monthly newspaper, the *Women Worker*. In 1905 she also helped to organise in London the Exhibition of Sweated Industries, which was designed to bring home to the general public the appalling conditions in which many of their co-citizens worked for tiny wages. One influential visitor to the Exhibition was the Princess of Wales, who was considerably moved by Macarthur's commitment to social justice.

Mary Macarthur was described as a vivacious and inspirational figure, someone who could put heart into people when they believed that all was lost. She was notable (in some eyes, notorious) for her effective support of women workers in a number of high-profile strikes, including those by the Cradley Heath Chainworkers in 1910 and the workers of the Millwall Food Preserving Company the following year. Affectionately known to many as "our Mary," her public appeal for one thousand loaves for strikers' families during the latter dispute produced an overwhelming popular response. During the Great War, her persistent advocacy of better treatment for workers in munitions factories brought her into sharp conflict with such pillars of the establishment as Lloyd George and Winston Churchill; but the final victory was hers when new statutory protections were introduced.

Mary's dynamic combination of moral courage and patience was particularly evident in her opposition to government proposals (favoured by many middle-class suffragettes) to extend the voting franchise to certain categories of better-off women while refusing it to those from less privileged backgrounds. While the government hoped that conceding a limited female franchise would take the steam out of the suffragette movement, Mary feared that such a move would set back indefinitely the granting of the vote to all adult citizens, irrespective of their social class or income. Pleading with her customary eloquence for female solidarity, she urged that it was better to wait for the day when all women would be allowed the vote than to divide their ranks by selfishly accepting a restricted franchise. By trying to move too fast, and grasping at whatever sops were offered by crafty politicians or employers, even the most courageous campaigners, Mary knew, could end up with second-best.[4]

The example of Mary Macarthur demonstrates how courage and patience, far from pulling in contrary directions, can significantly complement each other. It also shows that courage is not the special preserve of men. One target of her moral courage was precisely the prejudice that it was unfeminine for a woman to "act like a man" by standing up for herself or the things she believed in. The belief that if women or their interests needed protection, it was men's business to provide it, was not one that Mary and those like her could accept with equanimity. It took courage to show that courage was not exclusively a male virtue. But what Mary also helped to show is that courage need not mean aggressiveness, violence, intolerance of opposition, bravado or pitilessness to oneself and others. "Courage" of that description has little claim to be a virtue, for either men or women.

WHY TAKE RISKS?

If we ask, writes Jonathan Lear, "in the most general terms what it is about courage that makes it a human excellence, the answer, I think, is that courage is the capacity for living well with the risks that inevitably attend human existence" (Lear 2006: 121). Human life is risky because of our natural limitations: we are not all-powerful or all-knowing, we frequently cannot have what we want, and we are prone to form false beliefs about ourselves and our environment (2006: 119–20). It is true that we could reduce the risks we run by restricting our wants and minimising our contact with other human beings and their affairs; but then we would run the still more serious risk of reducing our lives to pointless nullity. Yet if it is courage that faces up to worthwhile risks, it is bravado that embraces risks *because* they are risks, usually in order to cut a dash or to satisfy vanity or *amour propre*.

The popular wisdom which holds that it is more characteristic of men – and particularly of young men – than women to take risks in order to "show off" has been broadly supported in recent years by social-psychological research. There is some experimental evidence to indicate that temperamental fearlessness, in both men and women, may be linked to low levels in the brain of a protein called corticotropin-releasing hormone (CRH). Research has found that when female mice with young are injected with CRH, they cower in fear when confronted with an aggressive male mouse, whereas untreated animals defend their nests vigorously. Speculation that the same chemistry operates in human beings has suggested the possibility of pharmaceutical uses of CRH-lowering drugs as a treatment for overanxiety and some cases of post-natal depression (Hopkin 2004).

A recent study by the psychologist G. William Farthing has explored the relative propensities of young men and young women to take physical risks by reference to so-called costly signalling theory (CST), which proposes "that displays of physical skill may be effective signals, particularly when the display is honest, by being truly costly or truly physically risks" (Farthing 2005: 172). CST develops an idea that has been around since the 1970s that "some cases of apparently frivolous risk taking by males may, in fact, serve the function of signalling the male's health and vigor to potential mates," so demonstrating their fitness to maintain and protect a family and the high quality of their genes (2005: 172). To test this hypothesis, Farthing asked 100 mixed-sex undergraduate students at the University of Maine to state their preferences for mates and friends among males and females who took or avoided risks across a range of closely specified situations. These were divided into two main groups, which Farthing labelled respectively "heroic risk items" (e.g. rescuing people from rivers or burning buildings, or intervening to protect the weak from bullies) and "nonheroic risk items," subdivided into "physical risk items" such as speeding or skiing, "drug-risk items" (e.g. alcoholic bingeing, eating hallucinogenic mushrooms), and "financial risk items" (e.g. gambling or buying risky stocks).

The results of Farthing's survey offered a partial confirmation of CST but also some surprises. Both male and female respondents preferred heroic risk-takers as both mates and friends, with females showing a more strongly marked preference than males. Farthing comments that "heroism – brave physical risk taking for the sake of other people – is clearly an attractive feature for a potential mate"; moreover, the benefit is likely to be "greater for females because her mate could defend both her and her children" (2005: 180). In regard to nonheroic risk items, in contrast (and contrary to the prediction of CST), women preferred risk-avoiders to risk-takers as mates, seemingly regarding men who engage in such activities as dangerous sports as needlessly imperilling their ability to look after the interests of their families. However, a further significant finding of the research was that most males falsely believed that women liked physical risk-takers as mates (2005:178–9). The startling mismatch between what men think women prefer in a mate and what they actually favour suggests that much male showy risk-taking to impress the female sex is worse than wasted effort, having an effect the reverse of that intended. But for males who engage in such behaviour there is some compensation in the fact that males in the survey expressed a strong preference for non-heroic physical risk-takers as same-sex friends: in contrast to women, who preferred to find their same-sex friends among physical risk-avoiders (2005: 180). (Neither sex, incidentally, had much liking for drug-risk-takers as either mates or friends.) Male bravado, in short, appears to impress the boys much more than it does the girls, whatever the former may believe.

If Farthing's research is reliable (and we need to be cautious about reading too much into the results of a single psychological study, especially one conducted on subjects from a relatively narrow cultural background), then useful light is thrown on the psychology of risk-taking behaviour and of attitudes to risk. But Farthing does not purport to provide a comprehensive account of the springs of courageous action. Proponents of CST do not claim that no one ever performs an heroic action unless it is to impress potential mates or friends. People who enter burning buildings to rescue a trapped child or dog probably rather rarely think of the kudos that they will earn; what matters to them is to save the endangered child or animal. Some daring deeds are anyway only possible under conditions of the greatest secrecy, where the right hand is not allowed to know what the left is doing (no medals were sought or given for protecting Jews during the Third Reich). Many evolutionary biologists believe that a disposition to perform altruistic acts is part of the natural endowment of human beings, a product of species evolution just as much as an aptness to take heroic risks with a view to impressing potential mates.[5] In any case, as rational moral agents we are capable of acting on ideals and values which transcend our self-concern. And we recognise that many of the things that enrich human life are only available if we are prepared to face what Lear calls "the risks that inevitably attend human existence" (Lear 2006: 121). This is a matter of taking risks not to look good but in order to do good.

In Lear's view, we are "erotic" creatures in the Platonic sense that "we reach out to the world in yearning, longing, admiration, and desire for that which (however mistakenly) we take to be valuable, beautiful, and good" (2006: 120). This may be a slightly over-romanticised conception, but there is no doubting the multiplicity of human desires and the difficulties that lie in the way of satisfying them, given our "lack of omnipotent control" and extensive talent for mistake and muddle. Courage is thus essential if we are not to remain chronically nonplussed by the risks that face us when we seek to realise our goals and live a happy life, and "the courageous person is someone who is excellent at taking those risks" (2006: 120, 121). To this we may add the Aristotelian thought that he is also excellent in taking those risks.

CARDINAL AND SPECIAL COURAGE

Because an interest in living well is obviously not restricted to men, courage must be an eligible and important virtue for women too. "Certain virtues," wrote a now largely forgotten but perceptive seventeenth-century moral philosopher, "are commonly called 'cardinal' because, like doors on their hinges, so on them all the honesty and sanctity of the moral life depends" (Eustachius a Sancto Paulo 1677: 109; my translation). These virtues include courage, which the same author thinks particularly noble since it seeks the fine and upright (and is therefore superior to temperance, which has the less exalted role of shunning the shameful) (1677: 133–4). This praise of courage anticipates Lear's claim that courage is a distinctive excellence of beings who yearn for the good, but it also looks back to St Thomas's remark that "the virtue of courage [fortitudo] has the task of protecting the human will so that it is not turned back through fear of bodily harm from the good proposed by reason" (Aquinas 1966: 15 [2a.2ae.123, 4]).

It was noted in Chapter 1 that Aquinas regarded courage as a cardinal virtue because the element of steadfastness is essential to the practice of *every* virtue. Aquinas did not mean that we must first be courageous before we can acquire any other virtue; his point was, rather, that courage is a constitutive principle of all virtues, a vital part of their make-up.[6] If our efforts to be (say) generous or truthful failed as soon as any obstacle or contrary temptation arose, then we could not truly be said to have those qualities. In fact, if such was our state of moral incompetence, we could make very little progress in living the good life in any recognisable form; our feeble efforts to realise any worthwhile goal would be so many futile misadventures. To vary the metaphor of doors and hinges, courage can also be thought of as moral backbone.

Aquinas carefully distinguished between courage as firmness of spirit (moral backbone) in general, and the more specific virtue of "enduring or repulsing whatever makes steadfastness outstandingly difficult; that is, particularly serious dangers" (Aquinas 1966: 9/11 [2a.2ae.123, 2]). Courage in the former sense was the cardinal virtue, and so, by implication, a component of courage in the latter, which Aquinas differentiated by saying that it was necessarily concerned with *fear* (understood rather broadly as an inclination to retreat in the face of any evil involving difficulty)(1966: 3 [2a.2ae.123, 3]). Aquinas implicitly recognised that both cardinal and "special" forms of the virtue are appropriate to both men and women. Although he followed Aristotle in citing the courage of soldiers facing death in battle as his main paradigm of the "special" virtue, he defined it quite broadly as the virtue that "is properly employed in sustaining all misfortunes" (1966: 15 [2a.2ae.123, 4]). Because death is the object of greatest fear to human beings, it follows for Aquinas that the most courageous are those who are not deterred from seeking some good by the danger of death. Thus a "brave man . . . does not shrink from attendance on a sick friend for fear of some deadly infection, or . . . from a journey on some matter of duty because of fear of shipwreck or bandits" (1966: 19 [2a.2ae.123, 6]).

Courage, then, whether cardinal or special, is not a virtue that more particularly pertains to one sex or the other. Yet inevitably there will be a certain amount of gendering of the virtue in actual social situations. In so far as men and women have different social roles (e.g. even today in most societies only men become fighting soldiers – and in all of them, only women undergo childbirth), the forms in which they are expected to manifest courage will vary. This need not be objectionable provided that role allocation is not determined on the basis of false or belittling assumptions about the kinds of courage of which men and women are capable. For Mr Giles and Pericles, little was to be expected of a woman, and nothing in the courageous line. One wonders what the Greek statesman would have made of Sophie Scholl, a leading figure in the White Rose movement whose activities we touched on briefly in Chapter 1. Executed at the age of twenty-two along with her brother and other group members for her unremitting efforts to stir up opposition to the Hitler regime, though knowing that these would ultimately cost her her life, Sophie Scholl has recently been voted by Germans one of their country's greatest women, an honour reflecting the degree to which, in the words of her biographers, "her simplicity, innocence and courage have caught the hearts of many" (Dumbach and Newborn 2006: xv). One might hope that even Pericles would have paid to Sophie the tribute that he paid to the Athenian dead: "The value of such a spirit is not to be expressed in words" (Thucydides 1994: 98 [Bk II, para. 42]).

Fortitude
Four

COURAGE AND FORTITUDE

Not very much is heard these days about fortitude, in contrast to courage. One could suspect that fortitude has gone the way of certain other once-popular virtues – chastity, sobriety and frugality are examples that spring to mind – and dropped out of moral fashion, for now or for good. But appearances may be deceptive here. Fortitude may not be much referred to by name by journalists, politicians, popular novelists or characters in soap operas, but it does not follow that the virtue itself has been forgotten; for fortitude may be present in the public mind *de re* even if it is not *de dicto*. Clearly this would be the case if fortitude were simply courage by another, more cumbersome name.[1] But while some writers have treated the terms "fortitude" and "courage" as virtual synonyms, an influential tradition has preferred to think of fortitude as an important species of courage rather than as the whole of it.

In the previous chapters I have generally used "courage" as a translation of the Latin *fortitudo* as well as of the Greek *andreia*, and have spoken of courage, rather than fortitude, as the cardinal virtue that partners justice, temperance and prudence. The justification for this is that the treatment of *fortitudo* in standard authors such as Aquinas encompasses a territory as wide as that covered in modern discussion of courage.

Nevertheless, courage and fortitude have frequently been differentiated along lines that were succinctly set out in the late nineteenth century by Henry Sidgwick:

> We generally denote by [Courage] a disposition to face danger of any kind without shrinking. We sometimes also call those who bear pain unflinchingly courageous: but this quality of character we more commonly distinguish as Fortitude.
>
> (Sidgwick 1907: 332)

While "a disposition to face danger of any kind without shrinking" is evidently one aspect of fortitudo as understood by Aquinas, Sidgwick notes that the English word fortitude has come to be used in a narrower sense than the parent Latin term (or the English term "courage" in its broadest usage).

Sidgwick's thumbnail definitions are more suggestive than precise and do not attempt to determine a firmer distinction between "courage" and "fortitude" than ordinary usage sanctions. The main difference between courage (in the narrower sense) and fortitude, as he understands them, is that the courageous person elects to confront rather than run away from some threatening danger, while the person of fortitude chooses to remain self-possessed in the face of adversity that has either arrived or will do soon. (I use the term "adversity" rather than "pain" since Sidgwick's definition of the virtue is patently too limited in this respect.) Other modes of drawing the distinction have emphasised more than Sidgwick does the active element typically involved in courage, the taking the war to the enemy rather than just sitting tight and awaiting his assault. The contrast has sometimes been characterised in terms of active and passive (or proactive and reactive) virtue, though this opposition can be overstated, since fortitude rarely involves no more than inertly taking misfortune "on the chin." According to the *Shorter Oxford English Dictionary*, while "fortitude" has the general meaning of "moral strength or courage," it is now used chiefly in the "passive sense" to mean "[f]irmness in the endurance of pain or adversity." On this account, fortitude's closest cousin among the virtues may seem to be not courage but patience (defined by the *Shorter Oxford* as "[t]he suffering or enduring (of pain, trouble, or evil) with calmness and composure"). This recalls Aquinas's view that patience is not merely related to the virtue that endures adversity but forms an integral part of it (Aquinas 1966: 91 [2a.2ae.128, 1]).[2]

Aquinas defines the "special," as distinct from the "cardinal," virtue of courage (*fortitudo*) as "firmness of mind in enduring or repulsing whatever makes steadfastness outstandingly difficult; that is, particularly serious dangers" (1966: 9/11 [2a.2ae.123, 2]). Although Aquinas's *fortitudo* covers both courage and fortitude as understood by Sidgwick and Oxford, his distinction between "*enduring and resisting*" those things which threaten our firmness shows him to have been thinking along not dissimilar lines. Holding that "the action of courage is twofold, attack and endurance" (*duplex fortitudinis actus*) (1996: 89 [2a.2ae.128, 1]), he proposes that to endure (*sustinere*) evils is a more basic (*principalior*) act of *fortitudo* than to attack (*aggredi*), because we must be able to repress our fears enough to hold our ground before we can entertain any serious thought of fighting back (1996: 21 [2a.2ae.123, 6]).

St Thomas's emphasis on endurance and standing one's ground (*immobiliter sistere in periculis*) as the foremost element in *fortitudo* was echoed centuries later in John Locke's definition of "[t]rue Fortitude" as "the quiet Possession of a Man's self, and an undisturb'd doing his Duty, whatever Evil besets, or Danger lies in his way" (Locke 1705: 199). Locke (for whom

"Courage" and "Fortitude" were synonyms) thought it vital to acquire early the capacity to endure the evils that are an inevitable feature of "an Estate, as ours is in this Life, expos'd to Assaults on all Hands." Fortitude of this sort should be taught to children of tender years, so that they would grow into adults of robust character, not liable to go to pieces at the first sign of trouble. For most people, Locke suggested, this was a more useful kind of courage than the more celebrated martial variety, since, honourable though that was, the ability to feel "Contempt of Life in the Face of an Enemy" was not much help in coping with the dangers that "attack us in other Places, besides the Fields of Battle" (1705: 198–200).

That fortitude of the required sort was a quality that "few Men attain to" was a sad fact that Locke attributed largely to deficiencies in their education. The way to handle children was to harden them gradually, encourage them to look on disgrace as a greater evil than physical pain, and "not to bemoan, or permit them to bemoan themselves, on every little Pain they suffer" (1705: 207). Locke's mode of child-rearing may sound severe by modern standards, but he insisted, too, that the child should be shown kindness and love. The idea was not to restore the over-rigorous discipline of ancient Sparta, which was vastly too harsh for the present age, but "by enuring Children gently to suffer some degrees of Pain without shrinking . . . lay a foundation for Courage and Resolution, in the future parts of their Lives" (1705: 206–7). By exposing the child to minor obstacles and discomforts, the Lockean educator prepared him to face the larger problems that would beset him in later life. The core of good sense to Locke's proposal is that overprotected children grow into under-protected adults, lacking the training that would enable them to stand reliably on their own two feet.

Locke's claim that fortitude as a capacity to endure evils (fortitude in the Sidgwickian sense) is rare may suggest that he saw it is an all-or-nothing virtue, rather than one that comes in degrees. Yet humankind cannot be neatly divided into those who are capable of enduring evils and those who are not. Many people possess a modicum of fortitude that is ample for coping with lesser evils though insufficient to sustain them when the going gets really tough. And a person who stands firm in one kind of situation (say, putting up with extreme cold) may be less well able to do so in another (say, living on starvation rations). Most people will also make more effort to summon up their fortitude when the welfare of loved ones is at stake, or cherished values need to be defended, than when a large investment of suffering will produce a return of little value. In the last case, to endure *à outrance* would not be fortitude but folly, or masochism.[3]

FORTITUDE AND THE SELF

The Latin adjective *fortis* means "strong" or "powerful," and we will not go far wrong if we follow this etymological clue and take fortitude to be a kind of strength. But precisely what sort of strength? One attractive answer is that fortitude – understood here as the "enduring" as distinct from the "attacking" form of courage – is the strength required for the preservation of the self. Strength is generally crucial to a thing's survival, or its maintenance of itself in its present state. Weakness is vulnerability, inability to withstand change, exposure to decay. Because we tend to admire strength (provided that it is not abused) and despise, or at best compassionate, weakness, we can value even the strength and firmness of such non-human objects as oak trees or the pyramids of Egypt (though of course we do not praise these as *agents*).[4]

Weak people, like trees liable to snap in the wind, are at the mercy of the elements; they go to pieces in stormy conditions. The strong, though they may need to bend with the breeze, retain their self-possession, and may even increase their moral and psychological integrity by the experience of hardship. Unlike the weak, they do not allow external forces to prove a solvent of the self.

It might be objected that selves are actually more resilient than this kind of talk suggests, and that even people who are conspicuously lacking in fortitude remain the same selves over time. So a person who behaved in a totally spineless fashion, constantly overwhelmed by her troubles, impatient, discontented and complaining, suffering but not enduring, would still retain her identity. (Indeed, her sharp sense that it was always *she* who, year after year, was dealt the bad hand in life's game might be a major intensifier of her misery.) But self-preservation, in the present sense, involves more than just keeping the self going; it means keeping it going in a healthy state. Fortitude may not be necessary for the bare survival of the self but it provides the stiffening when troubles come. Without fortitude, a person abandons her former goals and becomes absorbed in a sapping self-pity. The self remains, but it has become passive, yielding and directionless.

The role of courage of this sort in preserving the self has been well brought out by the German existentialist theologian Paul Tillich:

> One praises that in which a being fulfils its potentialities or actualizes its perfections. Courage is the affirmation of one's essential nature, one's inner aim or entelechy, but it is an affirmation which has in itself the character of "in spite of." It includes the possible and, in some cases, the unavoidable

sacrifice of elements which also belong to one's being but which, if not sacrificed, would prevent us from reaching our actual fulfilment. This sacrifice may include pleasure, happiness, even one's own existence. In any case it is praiseworthy, because in the act of courage the most essential part of our being prevails against the less essential.

(Tillich 2000: 4–5)

Tillich's point, in plainer language, is that in order to preserve the things that we stand for and which give us a sense that our lives are worth living, we may sometimes have to put our lives on the line. Self-preservation is not so much a matter of ensuring that we will continue to breathe, as of guarding against the things that threaten to destroy the meaning of our lives. Tillich may have had at the back of his mind the words of Jesus in the Gospel: "For whosoever will save his life shall lose it: but whosoever will lose his life for my sake, the same shall save it" (Luke 9:24). If the crucial thing is not to live but to live to some purpose or according to standards of excellence, then dying may sometimes be more self-preserving than living. Thus a martyr may choose to die rather than renounce her religious faith, a parent may throw herself in front of a speeding car to save her child, and a warrior may risk almost certain death at the hands of the enemy rather than beat an ignominious retreat. Tillich ascribes to Spinoza the insight that "[s]triving towards self-preservation or towards self-affirmation makes a thing be what it is," adding that such striving is "the essential act of everything that participates in being" (Tillich 2000: 20). Fortitude is a virtue because it is possible to affirm ourselves and show excellence of character even in the tightest, most unpleasant spots.

That preservation of the self requires one to be self-determining in the light of a certain conception of the good has been a leitmotif in the work of Alasdair MacIntyre. For MacIntyre, a successful life is like a coherently organised narrative, in which particular events gain their meaning from their place in the general plot line imposed by the author (the subject of the life). MacIntyre writes: "It is because we all live out narratives in our lives and because we understand our own lives in terms of the narratives that we live out that the form of narrative is appropriate for understanding the actions of others" (MacIntyre 1984: 212). Of course, none of us has complete control over the shape of his life: human histories interlock in complex ways and what happens in one person's story will usually affect many others. There is nothing to regret about this: as social beings, we should allow our personal stories to be dialogues and not mere monologues. Inevitably, much of our action is reaction to the actions of others. Yet we should strive to exert the ultimate authorial control over our own stories, shaping our own lives rather than having them shaped for us by others; and it often takes fortitude to keep the narrative on an acceptable track. A person who fails to react to adversity with fortitude effectively abandons the authorship of his own story; and if "[t]he unity of a human life is the unity of a narrative quest" for what the subject takes to be the good, as MacIntyre asserts, then his life now loses that unity (1984: 218–19). While MacIntyre believes that *all* the virtues assist in the subject's quest for the good, there is a strong case for ascribing fortitude a pre-eminent role, since without it the narrative quest would be halted at the first hint of trouble.

Yet there may seem to be a problem with the idea of fortitude as the primary virtue enabling us to keep the narrative of our lives on track. For isn't fortitude most needed precisely when we have lost authorial grip and need to make the best of whatever limited options are now available to us? In this view fortitude can seem an appropriate virtue chiefly for ex-authors. Think, for instance, of a person who has been forced into slavery and who no longer has any power of direction over his life. Being compelled to do what he is told, his story is essentially now one written by his master. Coping with the sad change in his condition from freedom to servitude undoubtedly requires fortitude, but it is the fortitude to come to terms with the fact that, as Aristotle puts it, a slave is no more than "a living tool" (Aristotle 1954: 212 [1161b]). Tools, though, are not engaged in any narrative quest for the good, and cannot need fortitude for that purpose.

But this objection is resistible. A slave may not control the overt plot of his life (unless he escapes, rebels or commits suicide) but provided that his conditions are not utterly dehumanising he can still direct the more important inner story. Both Socrates and the Stoics taught that human dignity can be amply maintained in undignified conditions so long as a person permits no compromise with vice. There may be an element of idealisation in this view, but there undoubtedly are character excellences open to slaves and prisoners who, while not free to do what they will, retain the capacity to be what they will. So a slave could choose to be cringing, whining, flattering and obsequious, or, instead, calm, resilient, uncomplaining, modest, veracious and cheerful. But to make the latter choice he needs to have, first of all, the fortitude to bear with his condition. Moreover, unless a slave or prisoner is kept in solitary confinement, he will interact with other human beings and have an influence for good or ill. The bars that keep a prisoner within may not be so effective at keeping nobility without. The fortitude of prisoners has sometimes taken stunningly heroic forms, as in the case of the Polish Catholic priest Maximilan Kolbe, who voluntarily died by starvation in Auschwitz in the place of another condemned prisoner who had pleaded for his life.[5] This was hardly the action of a man who had relinquished the authorship of his own narrative to someone else.

Fortitude, however, is consistent with differing degrees of control over the subject's personal narrative. Merely preserving the self from dissolution, though in very adverse situations it may be all that is attainable, is a relatively minimal form of fortitude, a moral and psychological holding operation which, though it may stave off disaster, does not compel misfortune to "add value" to the character. In its finest manifestations, fortitude not only sustains the self but presses adversity into the service of personal growth.

A notable example of such self-enhancing fortitude is found in Jane Austen's novel *Persuasion*, in the person of Mrs Smith, a lady formerly in affluent circumstances who has been reduced by a combination of ill-luck, injustice and illness to the condition of a housebound invalid, forced to do needlework to earn a meagre living. When the novel's protagonist, Anne Elliott, visits her former schoolfellow in her humble home, she marvels that Mrs Smith manages to maintain her spirits in spite of her cheerless situation:

> . . . Anne had reason to believe that she had moments only of languor and depression, to hours of occupation and enjoyment. How could it be? She watched, observed, reflected, and finally determined that this was not a case of fortitude or of resignation only. A submissive spirit might be patient, a strong understanding would supply resolution, but

here was something more; here was that elasticity of mind, that disposition to be comforted, that power of turning readily from evil to good, and of finding employment which carried her out of herself, which was from nature alone. It was the choicest gift of Heaven; and Anne viewed her friend as one of those instances in which, by a merciful appointment, it seems designed to counterbalance almost every other want.

(Austen 1986: 136; my italics)

Jane Austen's comment that "this was not a case of fortitude or of resignation only" implies a rather minimalist conception of fortitude which we do not need to follow; it corresponds to what I have described as fortitude of the "holding" variety which barely preserves the self but does nothing to add value. Mrs Smith's fortitude is of an altogether more active kind. The "something more" that she possesses beyond the mere power of putting up with ill-health, poverty and disappointment is a capacity to use her situation to enrich her own and others' lives. As she candidly admits to Anne, the sudden onset of a variety of misfortunes "had done her good," changing her from a giddy and thoughtless girl bent only on pleasure into a mature and self-controlled woman (1986: 136). This is the strength which begets strength; the increasing firmness of her character enlarges her own possibilities while it inspires a greater resilience in those, such as Anne, who benefit from her example. Mrs Smith's fortitude has significant analogies to that of the eponymous hero of Joseph Conrad's novel Lord Jim, who redeems his morally flawed self by willingly embracing a violent death. In Jim's case, it is the memory of a previous shameful failure of nerve that steels him to restore his integrity through a series of brave deeds culminating in a final act of sacrifice. Mrs Smith's career is less dramatic but she too discovers the strength to conquer rather than be conquered by difficult circumstances. Both ensure that the final authorship of their narrative remains firmly their own.

PATIENCE REVISITED

Possession connotes peaceful rule. So a man is said to possess his soul by patience in so far as he utterly uproots the feelings, aroused by hardships, which trouble the soul.

(Aquinas 1966: 195 [2a.2ae.136, 3])

As fortitude and patience are both concerned with facing up to adversity without making a fuss, there may seem to be little to distinguish them. Yet there is a case to be made for holding them to be distinct, if related, virtuous conditions. Fortitude is commonly found accompanied by patience, as it is in Mrs Smith, but the two states are not invariable associates. A clue to their difference is provided by the conventional unwillingness to speak of fortitude in connection with very trivial ills, though these may be borne with patience. The reason for this seems to be that patience has primarily to do with how one *feels*, while fortitude has most to do with how one *acts*; and the latter is generally more significant, to oneself and to others, than the former.

Aquinas, as so often, puts his finger on the nub: the patient person works on eliminating the disturbing feelings – grief, anger, hatred, hurt, envy – which the experience of hardship can arouse. While this attempt may be more or less successful, Aquinas emphasises that it would *not* be an exercise of patience merely to try to control these feelings and prevent their having any practical effect. The patient person aims to perform the "more perfect" act of uprooting them utterly, so restoring peace to her soul (1966: 195 [2a.2ae.136, 3]).[6] In contrast, someone who shows fortitude may lack the calmness of spirit which is the hallmark of patience; so she may meet a certain evil without quailing yet with emotions of intense anger or distress.

Fortitude and patience are apposite virtues when one is on the receiving end of troubles that one is unable to deflect, but they involve different kinds of strength: the subject of fortitude has the firmness of self-possession and endures hardship without flinching, while the patient individual has the power to dismiss such disturbing emotions as anger, bitterness, resentment, depression and disappointment. Patience, of course, like fortitude comes in degrees, and it would take the proverbial "patience of a saint" to preserve a perfect calm in every tranquillity-threatening circumstance. In fact, to maintain a complete absence of passion on all such occasions is very doubtfully virtuous, as it would seem to indicate an unhealthy degree of emotional disengagement from the world. Virtuous patience can best be regarded as a mean between impatience and total dispassionateness.

Since the measure of a person's patience is the extent to which she manages to rid herself of her disturbing feelings rather than the extent to which she keeps them in practical check, the latter, where it is called for, may more properly be considered an operation of fortitude. (Even if it is "more perfect," as Aquinas suggests, to eliminate disturbing feelings than to muzzle them, what mainly matters to others is what actions follow from those feelings.) Patience on a monument may smile at grief, but fortitude can indulge in the occasional grimace. Serious adversity is ideally met, as it was by Mrs Smith, with fortitude *and* patience.

Although patience can be manifested in regard to trivial

ills, it is by no means restricted to the sphere of minor evils. The displays of exasperation or annoyance that we designate as "impatience" are a far remove from those cases where a failure to attain tranquillity becomes a major threat to a person's self-possession. If Mrs Smith had wept and wailed about her fallen circumstances, she would have severely imperilled her ability to keep her life from shipwreck. A deficiency in patience may make it harder to sustain fortitude. Yet their dynamic relation is an intricate one. If allowing free rein to one's emotions can undermine one's ability to muster one's fortitude and make an effective stand against adversity, the presence of *some* degree of anger, resentment or sense of injustice may serve as a positive stimulus to hold one's ground. Too much placidity or meekness can be enervating, just as too much emotional upset can be unnerving. Someone who eliminates reasonable anger at wrong that is done him is in danger of becoming a cat's paw once it is discovered that evil does not ruffle his calm. Some people who are impressive for their fortitude are in fact conspicuously short on patience. Yet often the two are found together, since both appeal to the kind of temperament that values a cool, calm approach to difficulties and dislikes agitation and histrionics.

If patience, taken to excess, can lead to a fainéant attitude to evils that should not be put up with but opposed, fortitude – genuine fortitude, as distinct from a doltish insensibility to troubles – is less exposed to the same hazard. Recall Locke's characterisation of courage/fortitude as "the quiet Possession of a Man's self, and an undisturb'd doing his Duty" irrespective of besetting evils or dangers (Locke 1705: 199). For Locke, fortitude keeps us up to the moral mark, and as such is "the Guard and Support of the other Virtues" (198). It may sometimes be our duty to be patient, but patience is not, like fortitude, the virtue of doing our duty even in taxing circumstances. Preaching fortitude should therefore never be mistaken for enjoining passive submission to evils.

Here we should resist a variant understanding of fortitude, which draws it closer to patience. The Stoic Roman Emperor Marcus Aurelius's advice, in times of trouble, was to "withdraw into the little field of the self. Above all, never struggle or strain; but be master of yourself, and view life as a man, as a human being, as a citizen, and as a mortal." Because nothing that goes on outside the soul can really touch it, and "disquiet can only arise from fancies within," it is misapplied effort to work on the world when we can work on ourselves instead (Marcus Aurelius 1964: 64). Why bother to eliminate evil if it is possible to endure it?[7]

To which, the obvious riposte is: why strive to endure evil if one can eliminate it? Withdrawing into "the little field of the self" is in any case much harder than going home and closing the front door. For one thing, our sense of who we are is closely bound up with our value commitments, so a threat to our values is a threat to our self, and we cannot adequately defend the latter if we abandon the former. For another, since we live in the world, we cannot psychologically detach ourselves from everything that is going on around us and direct our gaze wholly inwards. Defending patience, Eamonn Callan remarks that "[i]t is only a puerile, coarse-grained patience that could motivate a blanket impassivity towards evils that are fit objects of determined resistance" (Callan 2005: 219). It would be a similarly crude and ill-judged fortitude that put up with evils that could and should be countered firmly.

Although we ought not to take resistible evils lying down, there are, sadly, many evils that we can do little or nothing about (old age, incurable illness, the death of loved ones, to name but three). Here, the main operation of fortitude is a stiffening of the will to exploit our remaining possibilities while enduring the evils which cannot be cured. This is quite different from displaying a lily-livered quietism in the face of those which can. And though it can be admirable to refuse to abandon a position that one knows one cannot ultimately hold, fortitude, like all virtues, needs to be tempered by practical wisdom; sometimes a gracious surrender to the inevitable is more fitting than a fruitlessly prolonged struggle. As Nancy Sherman has written, with acknowledgement to the Stoic Epictetus, "[w]e must learn where our mastery begins, but also where it ends" (N. Sherman 2005: 3).

SHOULD WE BE STOICAL?

The same Epictetus proposed that the key to living well could be summed up in two words, "endure" (*anechou*) and "abstain" (*apechou*). Fortitude (or to speak more accurately, a fortitude that was coupled with patience) and temperance were for him the two cardinal virtues because they concerned the things which were wholly within our power, our thoughts, sentiments, desires, aims and aversions; therefore it was a surer recipe for happiness to cultivate these virtues than to pursue things which we could never perfectly control (e.g. money, glory and political power). For Epictetus, who was born a slave in Phrygia around the middle of the first century, only our minds are truly free; and since "[W]hat upsets people is not things themselves but their judgements about the things," we should stop trying to mould the world to our own liking and focus instead on preserving our own tranquillity; for fortune can only be outrageous if we let ourselves be outraged (Epictetus 1983: 13). Not surprisingly, Epictetus's advice has often gone down well with soldiers and military personnel, who are heartened by his optimism about the resilience of the human will in times of trial. Epictetus was a favourite author of the nineteenth-century General Gordon of Khartoum and more recently has been popular with members of the US forces fighting in Vietnam and elsewhere.[8]

Yet there may be drawbacks to seeking to preserve our tranquillity come what may. Urging people to meet adversity with Stoic fortitude can seem worryingly close to telling them to shut down part of their humanity, as if the reactions that came naturally in times of trouble were something to be ashamed of. When Kipling writes in his well-known poem "If":

> If you can force your heart and nerve and sinew
> To serve your turn long after they are gone,
> And so hold on where there is nothing in you
> Except the Will which says to them: "Hold on!"
>
> (Kipling 1963: 273–4)

— you may then "be a Man, my son," but you may also be acquiring a rather smug self-satisfaction that causes you to look down on ordinary human fears and foibles, and by extension on those who display them. Fortitude often seems associated with a certain hard- or closed-heartedness, and may also sometimes breed it. A person who resolves to be pitiless towards his own pains is unlikely to pay much attention to the fears or feelings of others, and he may despise those who fail to reach his own high standards of firmness. Maintaining authorial self-control is a less admirable aspiration where one needs to sacrifice part of the self to do it.

Sometimes, inevitably, such firmness breaks down. In his life of the Stoic Cato the Younger, the Greek biographer Plutarch records that on the occasion of his brother's death,

"Cato showed the sensibility of a brother, rather than the fortitude of the philosopher. He wept, he groaned, he embraced the dead body; and besides these and other tokens of great sorrow, he spent vast sums upon his funeral" (Plutarch 1821: 245). Plutarch neither commends nor condemns Cato's unusual lapse from form, but it is clear that on his understanding of the virtue, men of fortitude, like big boys, don't cry. We, however, might think the worse of Cato if he *hadn't* cried.

Our modern ambivalence towards fortitude shows up in the difficulty we have in knowing how to respond to gallows humour and battlefield jokes. When, at the Battle of Lawfeldt during the Seven Years War (1756–63), the famously heroic and unflappable Brigadier George Townshend was standing next to a German officer who had his head blown off by a shell, the Brigadier nonchalantly wiped the bloody mess from his uniform, remarking, "I never knew that Scheiger had so many brains" (McLynn 2004: 207). Should we be more appalled at the callousness of Townshend's quip or admiring of his astonishing sangfroid under fire? Yet the callousness and the coolness are intimately connected, since such *sang-froid* can flow only from a *coeur-froid*. Someone with the characteristics of Townshend is clearly a man, in Kipling's sense; but is he also a human being of the kind we should look up to and emulate? And would he be a suitable role model for the youth of today?

Such questions arise because we are inclined to praise two seemingly opposite qualities: the strength which makes light of pains and troubles, and the softness which takes them seriously and seeks to administer help and consolation. One line in Kipling's "If" enjoins the young man to ensure that "neither foes nor loving friends can hurt you"; the next advises him to "let all men count with you, but none too much" (Kipling 1963: 274).[9] This sounds like the purchase of self-sufficiency at the cost of alienation not only from one's fellows but also from vital components of one's self. Not caring too much about hurting or being hurt may be useful for empire-builders, but it is less conducive to developing a person with lively sympathies and a capacity for love and friendship. Yet paying too much attention to avoiding anything which smacks of hardship or discomfort is also subversive of the self, because people who are over-concerned that the world shall not hurt them draw in their horns and live primarily in reactive mode, focusing on the evils they want to avoid rather than the goods that might be secured by taking some risks. It looks as if there is a golden mean between caring too much about adversity and caring too little, though determining where this lies in a given case calls for good judgement.

Ironically, attaching too little significance to adversity can undermine the very point of fortitude. If death, wounds, illness, bereavement, loss of goods or public reputation, disappointments and all our other tribulations are to be contemned as (in Stoic phrase) "things indifferent," then it is hard to see how there can be much merit in rising superior to them. This problem is not confined to the virtue of fortitude. Other virtues such as compassion, generosity, justice and tolerance lose their shine if the evils we combat when we exercise them are conventionally overrated. When Kipling proposes that Triumph and Disaster are "two impostors," and Stoics claim that vice is the only genuine evil, they come close to knocking virtue from its pedestal, contrary to their own intentions. If fortitude is about standing up to things that are only pseudo-evils, then it sinks to the status of a pseudo-virtue.

More defensible than genuinely disdaining adversity is treating it with what might be termed "methodological disdain," that is, pretending that evils are less significant than they are in order to make them easier to bear. Such methodological disdain need not depend on a morally dubious effort of self-deception. A person who has been diagnosed with terminal cancer may decide that the best way to prevent thoughts of impending death from poisoning her final days is to treat death *as if* it were unimportant. Although she knows this to be untrue, the device enables her to focus more attentively on the things that she still has to live for. Alternatively she might push thoughts of death to the back of her mind, refusing to dwell on them. (The difference between these is roughly that between making believe that an unwelcome guest is more congenial company than he is, and attempting to thrust him out of the door.) Arguably neither of these strategies is compatible with fortitude of the highest type, which fixes adversity with an unblinking gaze and refuses to be daunted by it. But both are consistent with the more modest kind of fortitude which admits of such prudential devices for maintaining self-possession.

It is sometimes hard to tell whether the appearance of contempt for death or other evils is sincere or methodological. La Rochefoucauld doubted whether any of the sages who professed to think death no evil genuinely believed what they claimed; the "wisest and bravest" are those who "make the best pretences" that death is indifferent but even they, he thought, are deluding themselves (La Rochefoucauld 1786: 28–9). Yet despite La Rochefoucauld's scepticism, some individuals do seem to have treated death with genuine lightness, either because (like Socrates and many Christians) they considered it a gateway to a better life, or, more bleakly, because it offered an exit from the trials of this one. This lightness, however, where death is judged to be either an indifferent thing or a positive good, should not be confused with fortitude.[10]

In his essay "On Tranquillity of Mind," Seneca relates the remarkable death of Julius Canus, an otherwise unknown Roman of the first century. Canus had the misfortune to fall out with the megalomaniac emperor Gaius Caligula and received his sentence of death from the tyrant's own lips; his only reply was, "I thank you, noble emperor." Seneca confesses himself puzzled as to what Canus meant by this "spirited reply": whether he accepted his sentence as a welcome release or was taunting the emperor with his cruelty or madness (Seneca 2005: 52). His account continues:

> Will you believe that Canus spent the ten days leading up to his execution without any anxiety at all? It is incredible what that man said, what he did, how calm he remained. He was playing draughts when the centurion who was dragging off a troop of condemned men ordered him to be summoned too. At the call he counted his pieces and said to his companion, "See that you don't falsely claim after my death that you won." Then, nodding to the centurion, he said, "You will be witness that I am leading by one piece."
>
> (2005: 53)

On the face of it, Canus's nonchalant acceptance of an unjust death could represent genuine contempt of death, methodological disdain, or mere doltishness. But Seneca explains that Canus was no blockhead but a philosopher keen to observe, at the moment of death, whether the soul was aware of leaving the body ("No one," he admiringly remarks, "ever pursued philosophy longer."). Nor was Canus's seemingly absurd concern about who won the game of draughts to be taken at face value:

> Do you think that Canus was just enjoying his game at
> that board? He was enjoying his irony.
>
> (2005: 53)

There is patently something studied about Canus's leaving of the world which makes the underlying psychology hard to pin down. The element of play-acting and the evident desire to leave a lasting impression of what Seneca describes as "serenity in the midst of a hurricane" may suggest that Canus's disdain for death was of the methodological variety, a deliberate attempt at self-distraction from the real horrors of his situation (2005: 53).[11] Treat dying as a game and you can pretend it to be a less important game than a contest at draughts. By turning his death into a piece of performance art, Canus may have made it easier to overlook its existential significance. Yet there would have been no need for pretence if he had really looked on death with the ironic, mocking eye that Seneca ascribes to him. If Canus thought human life (at any rate under the emperor Caligula) a poor thing, he may have regarded dying as no more significant than losing at draughts. But in that case what Seneca praises as his exemplary philosophical fortitude would be more appropriately commiserated as a regrettable, if understandable, world-weariness.

GENERAL GRANT

It should not be assumed that someone who does not (in J. L. Austin's phrase) "sing songs" in the face of death or other serious adversity must be treating it with either real or methodological disdain.[12] Fortitude does not require that we should make light of our troubles, or that we should try to suppress the emotions they naturally evoke in us. What it *does* demand is that we should have the willpower to stand firm and self-possessed in spite of them (the maintenance of a stiff upper lip being an optional extra). Fortitude at its best also needs no buttressing by pretence or evasion.

Fortitude of the highest order was displayed by Ulysses S. Grant, ex-general and former US president, in the final months of his life before his death from cancer in 1885, and his case affords a suitable study with which to close this chapter. Grant's previous history, remarkable though it was, need not much concern us here. His early career in the army, while showing evidence of his talents as a military strategist and commander of men, was brought to a premature close by alcoholism and depression, and subsequent failures in business only tended to confirm the common impression of Grant as a man whose character flaws outweighed his strengths. The outbreak of the Civil War in 1861, however, gave Grant the opportunity to redeem himself. Rejoining the Union army shortly after the commencement of hostilities, Grant, though not invariably successful in the field, caught the eye of Abraham Lincoln as a man with the ability, pluck and determination that was sorely lacking in most of the generals on the Union side. Promoted by the President to the highest command, Grant – whose slouching and untidy figure made a striking contrast to the aristocratic bearing of the Confederate General Robert E. Lee – eventually wore down the enemy in a series of hard-fought campaigns, and accepted Lee's surrender at Appomattox Court House in April 1865. Later, in 1868, he was elected as US President on a Republican ticket, but though he served two terms in that office, his presidency is generally judged to have been a lacklustre one, frequently marred by weak judgement and economic incompetence.

Following his presidency, Grant made a further attempt to succeed in business, but the collapse of Grant & Ward, the brokerage firm that he had founded in 1881, left him and his family bankrupt and with massive debts. No previous US president had ever gone broke, and Grant's situation, which could not be hidden from the public, was not only financially disastrous but acutely embarrassing. Yet, in the words of a recent biographer, "this very degree of humiliation laid the base for his last and greatest victory. He could treat his countrymen to another performance of heroism. He could publicly pull himself and his family up out of poverty" (McFeely 1982: 493).

Grant's rescue plan was to write and publish his personal memoirs, which would serve the twin objectives of recouping his finances and leaving a valuable record of the Civil War from his own unique perspective. But the task was scarcely begun before, one day in May 1884, Grant felt a severe pain in his throat while eating a peach. Medical examination revealed a cancerous tumour, which Grant's doctors judged already too advanced to be operable. In the ensuing months his condition worsened rapidly, and eating and speaking became intensely painful to him. Continually coughing and vomiting on account of his ulcerated throat, Grant worked doggedly at his writing, labouring to complete the book before he died – an event which he knew could not be very long delayed. A temporary improvement of his condition in January 1885 (when part of the tumour appears to have been dislodged as a result of haemorrhage) allowed Grant a little literal and figurative breathing space, but there could never be any doubt about the final outcome. Writing to his doctor shortly after, Grant admitted that he expected to die of "hemorage, strangulation, or exhaustion" (McFeely 1982: 505).

As Grant moved closer towards death, his family and friends begged him to write less and rest more; but the man who had fought the Civil War to the bitter end was unmoveable: the only thing that mattered now was to finish the memoirs, and it was pointless to jeopardise this objective for the sake of a few extra weeks of life. By now the American public was well aware of the General's last fight and was following its progress avidly. Crowds of well-wishers made the pilgrimage to the family's country home at Mount McGregor, New York, hoping to catch a sight of the dying hero seated on his porch. Grant finally died, aged 62, on 23 July 1885, having completed his book just nine days earlier. When the work was published in New York in two volumes in 1885–6, the *Personal Memoirs of Ulysses S. Grant* swiftly re-established the Grant family fortunes and was universally hailed as an historical document of prime importance.

Grant's impressive fortitude was less hedged about by psychological and moral ambiguities than that of Julius Canus, and the victor of the Civil War certainly faced death without "singing songs." As Grant maintained authorial control of the narrative of his own life to the very end, it is strikingly appropriate that his last months were devoted to the literal penning of his own story. Grant's fortitude ensured that his life would finish in the way he wanted it to, a way that would make up for many previous failures. It is true that Grant might have died before his book was completed; but that ever-present possibility was itself a stimulant to fortitude since it forced him to forego the usual comforts of a dying man. Hence it can fairly be said of him, as of Shakespeare's Thane of Cawdor (if for better reason), that "Nothing in his life / Became him like the leaving it."

Courage and Goodness

Five

"Lady Delacour and I were once great friends; . . . but she was too weak for me – one of those people that have neither the courage to be good, nor to be bad."

"The courage to be bad," said Belinda, "I believe, indeed, she does not possess."

Mary Edgeworth, *Belinda* (1986 [1801]: 20)

CAN WE COURAGEOUSLY DO WRONG?

"The courage to be bad" – whatever could that be? If courage is a virtue, then how could it ever be directed towards bad ends, as the speakers in this snippet from an early nineteenth-century novel evidently think possible? Recall Aristotle's view:

> But courage is noble. Therefore the end also is noble; for each thing is defined by its end. Therefore it is for a noble end that the brave man endures and acts as courage directs.
>
> (Aristotle 1954: 65–6 [1115b])

For Aristotle, courage, like any other virtue of character (*ethike arete*) is internally connected with the good. Accordingly, the virtuous person takes pleasure and pain in the things he ought, and "the good man tends to go right and the bad man to go wrong" in regard to these (1954: 32–3 [1104b]). It is possible that a person might set her mind on "going wrong" in spite of the attendant difficulties or dangers, e.g. social sanctions and disapproval, the pangs of her own conscience, or the rival attractions of the good. But if she does, she cannot then – a logical "cannot" – be acting with the virtue of courage. Either she is not acting with courage at all, or she is acting with something not envisaged by Aristotle, a non-virtuous form of courage.[1]

Gordon Brown begins his book on courage by remarking on his enduring fascination with people who put their lives or livelihoods on the line by standing up for the ideals they believe in (Brown 2007: 1). Jonathan Lear, we have seen, thinks courage a human excellence because it is "the capacity for living well with the risks that inevitably attend human existence" (Lear 2006: 121). We generally admire courage not just because it gets the job done but because it gets a good job done. The courageous individuals we most look up to are defenders of the right, eager to do what should be done notwithstanding the risks. They fit Aristotle's description of virtuous agents as people who do the right thing knowing it to be good and because it is good (1954: 34–5 [1105a–b]).

Call this the standard model of the courageous agent. But then, what should we say about the following cases that show considerable deviations from it:

(A) *the suicide bomber* who, to further his political or religious ends, explodes a bomb in a crowded marketplace, killing himself and many innocent civilians and seriously injuring many more;

(B) *the bold hit man* who, in return for a large cash payment, undertakes to assassinate the well-guarded enemy of a Mafia "godfather";[2]

(C) *the intrepid burglar* who, wanting to gain access without being seen to a building he intends to rob, approaches it from the rear across a dangerous broken-down bridge;

(D) *the daring youth* who, to prove his fitness to join the local gang, attempts to walk across the same perilous bridge?

Are any of these genuine instances of courage? And, if so, is the courage on display *virtuous* courage?

Superficially these resemble any other questions that ask whether something is the case or not. But asking about the nature of courage is not quite like asking about the molecular structure of water, or the rules on income tax, or the composition of the House of Lords. These are questions with determinate answers, to be found by appropriate investigation of the facts. But the questions about courage are different, because here the task is less to discover what courage is than to decide what we want it to be. Exactly the same goes for other virtues, and for virtue in general. Virtue concepts have the boundaries we fix for them, which requires us to ponder the kinds of action we wish to promote or discourage. Any attempt to say what courage or any other virtue is involves an unavoidable element of persuasive definition.

Choosing among the disconcertingly different definitions on offer is not easy. Some authors follow Aristotle and favour a morally "thick" concept of courage which treats directedness on the good as an essential feature of this (as of any) virtue. On a view of this kind, none of the cases (A) through (D) will count as examples of the virtue of courage. Others have been content with "thinner" conceptions which drop the insistence that the end should always be good, though expecting it to be so normally; some qualify this position by holding that the courageous agent must at least *believe* the end to be good. But some conceptions are wholly neutral on the moral status of the ends to which courage may be directed. On these views, the pretensions of (A) to (D) to be cases of courage will not be questioned on moral grounds, whatever may be said about their practical (ir)rationality. It might be thought that by breaking the linkage with goodness altogether, such views could no longer claim courage to be a *virtue* – unless they understood virtue in general in a similarly thin way, as something like a class of merely instrumental skills. But, as we shall see, a case can be made for regarding courage as a morally admirable quality in *itself*, irrespective of the moral status of the ends it serves.

Here an analogy with physical strength may be helpful. While physical strength is reasonably thought of as a good thing (much better than physical weakness), it is obviously capable of being employed for bad ends. And just as we can distinguish between good and bad applications of physical strength, we can also distinguish between good and bad applications of courage (what some medieval writers referred to as *fortitudo bona* and *fortitudo mala*). To talk of someone showing a commendable courage on some occasion therefore needs disambiguation: for it is possible that his courage, though fine and praiseworthy in itself, has been wrongly, even deplorably, applied. Deciding what kinds of courageous behaviour we want to encourage is part of a broader enterprise of framing an ethical outlook, for which we need an account of admirable courage (*fortitudo bona*) which coheres with, enhances and sustains other components of a practical blueprint for living well in a difficult world. Such a blueprint needs to be informed by what John Rawls has called a "conception of the good," a view, or vision, of worthwhile ends and values that provides us with crucial existential pointers (Rawls 1972: *passim*). And while it would be wrong to think that there must be one "best" or "correct" conception of the good, there is scope for evaluating rival ideals of courageous behaviour on the basis of their fit with the conception or conceptions we find most attractive.

By distinguishing the value of courage and of its applications, we can recognise the moral difference between the bold behaviour of the hit man of case (B) and that of Sophie Scholl in her anti-Nazi activities. Both display a quality of courage that merits praise. But there the resemblance ends. For while the hit man misapplies his courage in carrying out the evil wishes of his Mafia boss, Sophie puts her life on the line for the far worthier purpose of combating an horrific regime. Both Sophie and the hit man have the admirable quality of courage, but only one of them applies it admirably. Sophie's courage is the finer of the two in the sense that it is devoted to better ends.

Taking a morally thick line on courage can also lead to withholding credit where credit is due in less controversial cases than that of the hit man. We saw how Aristotle's exceptionally thick concept of the virtue implied its absence in any but soldiers on the battlefield, and denied it even to many of those: trained mercenaries were not truly brave, since they ran small risks in combat, nor were conscripted men who had no choice but to be where they were; only those who willingly ran the risk of death because it was noble to do so could properly be ascribed the virtue (Aristotle 1954: 64–6 [1115a–b], 67–8 [1116a–b]). Aristotle's reluctance to allow courage to any but a few reflects his wish to associate the virtue only with the noblest spirits; but the result is ungenerous, and suggests that he has attached too many strings.

In his *Profiles in Courage*, John F. Kennedy takes a less grudging view of courage, holding that men can be brave on both sides of a conflict such as the American Civil War, even though at most one side's cause can be right. "Surely," says Kennedy, "in the United States of America, where brother fought against brother, we did not judge a man's bravery under fire by examining the banner under which he fought" (Kennedy 1964: 211). Confederate soldiers were no less brave than Union men, and Robert E. Lee no less honourable than Ulysses S. Grant, notwithstanding the fact that the South was defending slavery. Many people would probably give this sentiment a nod of approval; in a civil war, where brother fights brother, it seems invidious to ascribe one side a monopoly of courage. Yet matters may seem less clear-cut where a sense of brotherhood is more elusive. Consider the fanatical Nazi storm trooper who risked death in the service of his Führer, or the Afghan jihadi who selflessly takes on superior forces for the sake of his religion, or the suicide bomber of case (A). Do all these individuals exhibit true courage, or only one of its simulacra? Are there no limits at all to the banners under which *brave* men and women can serve?

"BAD COURAGE": FOR AND AGAINST

A survey of the literature on the relation of courage to goodness reveals an extent of disagreement unusual even for philosophers. Plato even disagreed with himself, changing his view in the course of his career. His early dialogue *Laches* canvasses a number of definitions of courage but closes with the candid admission that the virtue remains mysterious, its precise analysis defeating even the subtle wit of Socrates. The discussants in *Laches* do, though, agree that courage is noble, and Socrates argues that someone who does bold but foolish things (such as diving into a cistern when one has no skill in diving, or staying at one's post on the battlefield long after there is any good to be gained by it) cannot be courageous, since folly can never be noble (Plato 1953a: 87–9

[192c–193e]). A different tack is taken near the end of the dialogue, where it is suggested that courage is "the knowledge of the grounds of hope and fear"; but this too fails, thinks Socrates, because such knowledge is more plausibly seen as coextensive with virtue in general than with courage in particular (1953a: 93–7 [196d–199d]).

Even the seemingly firm assumption that courage, whatever else it may be, is always *noble* has disappeared in Plato's later dialogue the *Statesman*. Here the main protagonist, the figure known as the "Eleatic Stranger," urges that bold spirits should never marry other people like themselves but instead mate with temperate, orderly ones. Where this eugenic advice is not heeded, "courage, when untempered by the gentler nature during many generations, may at first bloom and strengthen, but at last bursts forth into downright madness" (Plato 1953c: 529 [310d]). Meanwhile temperance, with too little bolstering by courage, will decay after several generations into listless enervation. Therefore, thinks the Stranger, the best rulers have both temperate and courageous elements in their ancestry; they combine justice and caution with "that restless energy which achieves its object" (1953c: 530 [311a]). Serious problems arise when courage occurs without a leaven of temperance, for of its own nature the courageous soul is uninterested in justice and "inclined to brutality" (1953c: 528 [309e]). Since brutal acts obviously have nothing of the noble about them, it appears that the Plato of the *Statesman* takes a morally thinner view of courage than the Plato of the *Laches*.

To move from Greece to Rome, Cicero in his book on duties (*De Officiis*) insisted that courage was essentially governed by the rules of justice, and approvingly cited the Stoic doctrine that courage is "that virtue which champions the cause of right." A bold and adventurous mind which is

"inspired not by public spirit, but by its own selfish purposes" should therefore be described as showing "effrontery"
(*audacia*) and not courage (Cicero 1961: 65 [Bk 1, ch. 19]).
For Cicero, there was no such thing as *fortitudo mala*.

Echoing Aristotle and the earlier Plato, Paul Tillich asserts
that "[c]ourage does what is to be praised and rejects what is
to be despised." Courageous action aims at the most exalted
goals, and in striving for these courageous people affirm their
essential nature and bring their own perfection closer. "It is
part of the beauty and goodness of courage," writes Tillich,
"that the good and the beautiful are actualized in it" (Tillich
2000: 4–5). Other philosophers have maintained a similar
line, if not always in such high-flown language. Thus Josef
Pieper argues that courage, like the other cardinal virtues,
promotes the "actual good of man," his "self-realization in
accordance with reason"; therefore "a 'fortitude' which is
not subservient to justice is just as false and unreal as a 'fortitude' which is not informed by prudence"; the cardinal virtues, in other words, can be expected to stick together (Pieper
1966: 125). And Douglas Walton contends that our contemporary concept of courage contains an element of positive
evaluation, so that:

> Anyone who tried to define "courageous" act as "an act done
> by an agent as a necessary means to some end" would
> produce an inadequate and incorrect definition if he failed to
> add the normative requirement that the end be good and the
> means formidably dangerous or difficult.
>
> (Walton 1986: 79)

Unless we insist that its end be good for an act to be courageous, it will be "hard to justify the thesis that courage is a
virtue worthy of high regard" (Walton 1990: 230).

Philippa Foot likewise thinks that there is "more difficulty than might appear in the idea of an act of injustice which is nevertheless an act of courage," and that we are right to have qualms about describing plucky but villainous acts as "courageous" (Foot 2002: 15). Peter Geach acknowledges the difficulty, holding that "there can be no virtue in courage, in the facing of sudden danger or the endurance of affliction, if the cause for which this is done is worthless or positively vicious" (Geach 1977: 160). But both these writers are prepared to consider a possibility rejected by some others, namely, that bold but wicked acts could still manifest a kind of courage, albeit of a degraded and non-virtuous sort.

By contrast with the previous writers, Kant saw no conceptual strain in the idea that such "qualities of tempera-ment" (*Eigenschaften des Temperaments*) as "courage, resolution, perseverance," while "good and desirable in many respects," might "become extremely bad and mischievous" when in the service of a bad will (Kant 1909: 9) – though it arguably sidesteps the problematic issue to label the traits in question as psychological qualities rather than "virtues." Arthur Schopenhauer expressly denied that courage was a virtue, seeing it as a morally neutral disposition with no necessary direction on the good. While courage often leads to fine results, "it is just as ready to serve the unworthiest ends" (Schopenhauer 1970: 134). A century later, G. H. von Wright maintained that burglars who run considerable risks in carrying out their audacious crimes may be acting with great courage, though they act "much to the detriment of their neighbours' welfare" (von Wright 1963: 53).[3]

James Wallace holds that "[e]very courageous act must have some aim or end that the agent has reason to regard as important or worthwhile" but allows that this objective need not be morally good: "one can act from motives that are morally reprehensible and still show courage" (Wallace 1978: 76, 77). Unlike, for instance, honest or generous acts, which are characteristically motivated by the agent's honesty or generosity, courage is not itself a motive but, rather, "a virtue that is shown in acting for other ends or goals" (Wallace 1978: 77) – which might on occasion be very bad. Per Bauhn similarly contends that "[c]ourage *may* serve morality, but this is not a matter of logical or empirical necessity" (Bauhn 2003: 39). And William Miller, while noting that "[c]ourage has a special cachet. People care about it desperately," describes it as "a gray virtue, equally serviceable for good and bad causes" (Miller 2000: 8).

An intermediate position has been taken by Daniel Putman, who proposes that, for an act to count as courageous, the agent needs to *believe* it to be morally worthy, and not merely good for her, even if that belief should be mistaken. "Though not sufficient for courage," he writes, "confidence in the worth of the cause is a necessary condition of courage" (Putman 2001: 464). Putman would agree with Kennedy that intrepid fighters on the Confederate side in the Civil War counted as brave; and he would presumably ascribe courage to the suicide bomber of case (A). But his view excludes from the honoured band the bold hit man and the intrepid burglar of cases (B) and (C), who could scarcely have believed that their actions served estimable or even minimally acceptable ends. It would also exclude the daring youth of case (D), unless he viewed his act as morally fine as well as personally profitable.

THE INTRINSIC WORTHINESS OF COURAGE

The foregoing brief survey of the literature on courage and goodness shows how highly divergent are the views on offer. The idea explicitly favoured by Wallace and Miller, and hinted at by Kant, is that courage is a morally admirable disposition of the will in *abstraction* from the ends which it serves. By adopting this line, proponents of morally thin conceptions of courage which allow cases such as (A) to (D) to count as courage in spite of their morally questionable objectives can restore some moral content to the virtue by positing the moral admirableness of the firm disposition of the will in face of danger. This way, courage can be esteemed not merely as a kind of executive skill but also as a genuine moral quality. The intrepid burglar of case (C) now merits praise for his bravery as well as blame for his thieving: a more nuanced appraisal which, I suggest, is in better accord with common moral intuitions than the wholly damning judgements implied by some other conceptions of courage.

Until they fall under the spell of certain philosophers, many people feel little strain in acknowledging that there is something admirable in an intrepid burglar that is lacking in an opportunistic sneak thief. "What a pity," they might say, "that so-and-so didn't employ his courage in a better cause." Given the crooked timber of which, as Kant famously remarked, human beings are made, it is not surprising that genuine qualities of character are occasionally found in the service of bad ends. Those who reject the possibility of "bad courage" will no doubt insist that morally good qualities cannot give rise to bad actions. But in the burglar's case, it is not his courage which leads him to pursue bad ends but his dishonesty, his imperfect sense of "meum" and "tuum." Although his courage assists him to secure his aim, it has no tendency in itself to make him a burglar. When Aristotelians assert that a person can never be nobly moved to pursue ignoble aims, they should bear in mind that what drives the burglar's enterprise is not courage but greed.

BAUHN AND FOOT ON "BAD COURAGE"

The claim that courage can be evaluated in abstraction from the ends it serves explains, if true, how courage can still be a praiseworthy moral virtue even where, as in the hit man's or burglar's cases, it supports morally bad action. Biting the bullet and accepting that morally commendable courage can combine in practice with morally censurable action has the added advantage of enabling us to discard a number of unsuccessful arguments that have been put forward to deal with the problem of "bad courage." Since some philosophers have found these persuasive, they are worth glancing at here, though none, I shall argue, is ultimately compelling and their failure can be looked upon as an additional reason for adopting the "abstractionist" view of Wallace and Miller.

In *The Value of Courage*, Per Bauhn claims that many people feel embarrassed about calling the bolder kinds of villain "courageous." Their reluctance to apply the epithet to them stems from the fact that "courageous" is a term of praise, "and we are not disposed to lavish praise on people we despise" (Bauhn 2003: 38). At the same time, we do look upon such men as Alexander the Great or King Richard III as "undoubtedly courageous," even though "from a moral point of view, they [were] flawed by character traits such as vanity and ruthlessness." Bauhn proposes that the best way to reconcile these conflicting attitudes is to regard the word "courageous" as a term, in some contexts, of *prudential* rather than of *moral* praise. So when we call a villain courageous, we mean that he or she is someone "who gets things done, even in the face of adversity"; bad people with courage have "the ability to perform even under difficult psychological circumstances" (2003: 38).

Bauhn's proposal is unsatisfactory. To start with, his characterisation of a "prudential value" as "a good that enhances our capacity for successful agency" (ibid.) is excessively general and fails to pinpoint anything that is distinctive about prudence as normally understood (it also implies that such natural goods as sharp eyesight or physical strength, which likewise assist successful agency, will count among prudential values!). Absent from Bauhn's formulation is any reference to prudence as the virtue – or more neutrally, the trait – that is more likely to keep us out of trouble than to get us into it (Philippa Foot remarks that prudence "inspires many a careful life" [Foot 2002: 17]). Prudent people are typically cautious and discreet rather than bold and daring, accustomed to look before they leap (though a virtuous person will not allow prudence to degenerate into cowardice). Prudence in this sense is not a quality we readily associate with bold and unscrupulous go-getters such as Richard III or Alexander the Great. Nor does the gangster, burglar or ram raider who chooses a highly risky career in preference to a steady nine-to-five job appear a shining example of laudable prudence.

But perhaps this objection should not be pressed too far. For Bauhn has probably chosen the word "prudence" imprudently. His point is not really that bold villains can be praised for their prudence, but that they deserve credit for their ability to get things done in spite of difficulties and dangers. This amounts to ascribing to them a certain kind of executive skill (though this term does not by itself quite cover the element of "will-do" that complements and activates the "know-how").

More problematic for Bauhn, however, is the implication of his view that the term "courage" in common parlance is ambiguous, sometimes referring to a moral quality and sometimes to a practical capacity. The claim that the term "courage" in English is systematically ambiguous is hard to credit, and will come as a surprise to ordinary speakers, who are normally unconscious of using a word with two distinct meanings. Bauhn's desire to find *something* praiseworthy about the actions of a man like Richard III stems from his reasonable reluctance to abandon the idea that a person who is undeterred by difficulty or danger has something estimable about him. Since he cannot be praised for his dauntless pursuit of the good, then he must, thinks Bauhn, be laudable instead for his ability to get things done in the face of adversity. And so he might; but it can only be confusing to use the same adjective "courageous" to carry both meanings. Aristotelians will refuse point-blank to call the wicked bold agent "courageous" or "brave."[4] But those who are willing to bestow on him the epithet will see themselves as ascribing the same praiseworthy quality as when they use the same word of a worthier agent. If we are prepared to call the assassin of case (B) "courageous," it is because he impresses us in the same way as does a well-intentioned person who takes similarly large risks in a better cause. It also shows that we are distinguishing between the moral qualities of ends and agents in the manner envisaged by Wallace and Miller. While the bravery of the murderer in no way mitigates the heinousness of the crime, this quality in the murderer attracts esteem in abstraction from the moral character of the intended objective; the bravery shown is good, even though the deed that is bravely done is bad.

A second conceivable way of evading embarrassment over the notion of "bad courage" is to suppose that in some people courage is not a virtue, moral, intellectual or executive, but a wholly bad thing, meriting only censure. According to Philippa Foot, courage is not alone among qualities normally thought of as virtues that have, in some people's case, "a systematic connexion with defective action rather than good action." In a person who is consistently over-industrious or has a horror of pleasure, for instance, industriousness or temperance might be held to be vices rather than virtues (Foot 2002: 17). This line would allow us to deny that a virtue ever serves bad ends, and to assert that the courage shown by the suicide bomber, the intrepid burglar or the bold hit man is not that disturbing thing, a virtue put to bad use; rather, in him it is not a virtue at all (though it is genuine courage).

As Foot herself acknowledges, this account soon comes to grief, since there are agents in whom courage variously gives rise to good and bad actions (2002: 16). The daring burglar may one day rescue a child from a burning building, so refuting the generalisation that courage in him is always a vice. While it may be regrettable that a person whose bravery produces more harm than good was not born with a more timorous character, his occasional good brave deeds rule out describing him as someone in whom courage is vicious.

The notion of *vicious* courage is also inconsistent with the idea — if we endorse it — that courage possesses a core of positive moral value regardless of the ends to which it is put. A brave villain may have multiple vices, but he also has one redeeming quality not possessed by a cowardly, sneaking one (even though an agent who pursues a bad end bravely may wreak more havoc than one who goes more half-heartedly and cautiously to work). Courageous villains have the potential to do much good if only they would redirect their firmness of will to better ends. They go wrong not because they lack a virtue but because they misapply it.

The failure of this attempt to solve the problem of "bad courage" prompts Foot to float an alternative and more interesting proposal. An intrepid murderer who kills for gain, she concedes, is not a coward. Even so, she thinks, we would not want to call what he does "courageous" or "an act of courage" in view of the note of commendation conveyed by those expressions. It would be better to say that the act "took courage" (2002: 16). This may seem to be a distinction without a difference, and many speakers of English would probably jib at the notion that an act could "take courage" yet not be, by that token, "courageous." But Foot's proposal does not rely on disputable claims about the niceties of English usage. Its nub is that virtues do not always in practice function *as* virtues, and that when a virtue lacks its "characteristic operation" it may give rise to evil instead of good. So while the intrepid murderer performs a deed that takes courage, courage is not in this instance "operating as a virtue." Because it is only when they are operating in their characteristic mode that virtues merit praise, we can now, thinks Foot, accommodate at once our willingness to concede that the murderer has courage and our reluctance to find that courage commendable (2002: 17).

Yet what exactly does it mean to say that a virtue is "not operating as a virtue"? Foot's brief explanation is that virtues, when operating characteristically, tend to give rise to "good actions, and good desires." (It is not quite clear whether "characteristically" means simply "on most occasions" or is meant to refer to some intrinsic directedness-on-good that virtues possess; if the latter, then the act of an intrepid murderer would represent not just an untypical variety of courage but a perversion of it.) To clarify the idea of a virtue which does not operate as a virtue, Foot argues that there is an analogy between virtue terms such as "courage" and words such as "poison," "solvent" and "corrosive" which name properties of physical things. If P is a poison, "it does not follow that P acts as a poison wherever it is found." Sometimes it will be quite natural to say that "P does not act as a poison here," even though P is a poison and P is currently acting. In the same way, the courage of the murderer is not acting as a virtue when he turns it to nefarious ends (2002: 16–17).

This analogy and the analysis it rests on cannot withstand close inspection. It is far from clear what it can mean for P to be "acting, but not as a poison" if this is to bear any resemblance to the way in which the murderer's courage is acting. For the murderer's courage is still acting as the virtue of courage in the sense that, were this quality absent and the agent suffering from cold feet, there would be no murder. P might be said to be "acting, but not as a poison" if, for instance, it dyes a piece of fabric green. This effect evidently relies on the chemical properties of P but has nothing to do with the fact that P is also a poison. Yet the accomplishment of the murder does have everything to do with the fact that the agent is acting with the virtue of courage. To preserve the analogy, we would need to think of a case where P's action depended on its being a poison, while at the same time it was not acting as one.

But this is not easy, since it would be perverse to describe something as a poison in a context in which it had no poisonous effects, not for some merely accidental reason such as the subject ingesting too little of the substance to be harmful, but because it was not "operating as a poison" at all. The term "poison" is implicitly relativistic, and to say that P is a poison

Courage and Goodness

is really an elliptical way of saying that P is poisonous to such-and-such subjects in so-and-so circumstances. For instance, atropine, which is present in deadly nightshade plants (*Atropa belladonna*), is poisonous to human beings but not to rabbits. It would be odd to say, "Atropine is a poison, but it doesn't operate as a poison when rabbits ingest it"; rather, for rabbits, which can consume large quantities of deadly nightshade without ill effects, it is not a poison at all. One species' poison is another species' meat. (It would be equally inapposite and linguistically speciesist for a community of talking rabbits to say, "Atropine is a harmless substance, but it doesn't operate as a harmless substance when humans ingest it.") It is true that some substances *would* poison certain creatures if they lacked immune mechanisms (e.g. the ability to produce suitable chemical antidotes). But even here it would be wrong to say that the substance "is a poison but not operating as such" – for it *is* operating as such, only its operation is blocked. In the case of the intrepid murderer, we might similarly say that courage *is* operating as a virtue, only it is blocked (by the murderer's bad motives) from having any of its characteristic good effects. Foot's claimed analogy between virtue terms like "courage" and "poison" fails, therefore, to yield the result she wants.

AGAINST THE UNITY OF THE VIRTUES

It would be nice to think that all human talents, gifts and excellences were internally connected to the noble, but such thinking, as Kant recognised, would be wishful rather than realistic. It is not generally true that something that is, as Kant puts it, "good in many respects" is not operating as itself where it serves a bad end. The beauty of the sirens' singing lured sailors to their deaths but it would be strange to claim that it could not therefore have been "operating as music" when it was precisely its capacity to ravish the ear that made it so lethal. A person blessed with a lively wit who employs his talent to poke fun at others morally abuses a natural gift but also exemplifies a characteristic use of it. Take Winston Churchill's condescending quip about Labour Prime Minister Clement Attlee: "Mr Attlee is a very modest man. Indeed he has a lot to be modest about." We can hardly deny this to be genuinely witty just because it is (if rather mildly) malicious. But doing so would be analogous to denying that a bold act done with a bad purpose could be truly courageous. Neither denial seems justified except from the perspective of a misguided moral idealism.

It might be objected that courage, unlike wit or musical talent, belongs to the genus of *moral* excellences, which are characterised by a firmer internal connection with the noble. Yet recall Plato's claim in the passage quoted earlier from the *Statesman*, that particular excellences (*aretai*) require a moderating admixture of others if they are not to do at least as much harm as good. Courage without temperance can manifest itself as brutality, and temperance without courage as torpor. Courage without justice is also, for obvious reasons, a dangerous disposition. Amélie Rorty, developing this Platonic theme, remarks that virtues have a tendency to be expansive, ramifying "to develop and exercise associated supportive traits, while inhibiting other, often highly beneficial traits" (Rorty 1988: 316–17). Often the problem is not that the will is wicked or even weak, but that it is operating defectively because insufficiently informed by reason or enlarged by sympathy. So generosity can cause others to be overdependent on us, justice make us hard, candour produce hurt feelings, friendliness become favouritism and forgivingness softness. (Note that this is not quite the same claim as Aristotle's that *excessive* forms of virtues are vices. For a person may have the right amount of that quality the having of which constitutes the virtue and still do harm if the will is imperfectly disposed through a failure of practical reasoning, or a lack of the imaginative ability to put herself in other people's shoes, or a shortfall in some other, moderating virtue.)

It is a commonplace that people may be more impressive exemplars of certain virtues than of others. But is it possible to have some moral virtues and lack others entirely? According to what is known as the "weak unity of the virtues" thesis, this is impossible because, in the words of Rosalind Hursthouse, having a virtue involves "practical wisdom, the ability to reason correctly about practical matters," and practical wisdom "does not exist in discrete, independent packages, peculiar to each virtue, allowing . . . for the possibility that someone might be, for example, courageous but totally lacking in temperance" (Hursthouse 1999: 154). Even conceding the fact that a person who is notable for one virtue may be "pretty limited" in another (a fact implausibly denied by stronger versions of the unity thesis), an agent who manifests a particular virtue can be identified as "a certain sort of person all round" – a virtuous person "all the way through" or "deep down" (1999: 156). This view harks back to the Platonic idea (floated, we saw, in *Laches*, and recurring in other dialogues), that all virtue might be identified with a kind of knowledge, namely knowledge of the good and how to attain it. On this conception, to suppose that someone might have one virtue but not another is self-contradictorily to ascribe and yet deny him this knowledge. But to this it might fairly be objected that not only is it possible to know some things without knowing all, but that to equate virtue with know-ledge is to over-intellectualise it, ignoring entirely the all-important factor of will.

Hursthouse admits that people do sometimes appear to have some virtues and lack others. But their behaviour, she thinks, puzzles us; we feel that something does not add up.[5] When we investigate such cases more closely, we generally find that we have missed something, or been misled by appearances. We might discover that we had been over-estimating the goodness of the agent's character, or that on some occasion when she acted badly she was beset by an especially irresistible temptation or mistakenly believed that she was acting well (1999: 156).

It is true that we might do one of these things. But it is equally true that we might not. In the end we may be forced to conclude that a person who is courageous or charitable just is indifferently honest or truthful, or ineluctably vain or jeal-ous, or sexually predatory. The unity of the virtues thesis, even in its weak version, seems too readily and frequently refuted by experience to be credible to anyone who has not made an *a priori* decision to believe it. Hursthouse's contention that, if only we probe carefully enough, we should normally be able to locate an underlying unity below the surface appearance of virtue dissonance seems another case of wish-ful thinking, coloured by an over-romanticised view of human nature. It ignores what Rorty has rightly referred to as "the manifest independent variability of the . . . virtues" (Rorty 1988: 308), human agents' chronic non-compliance with the neat and orderly model of ethical behaviour beloved by unity theorists.[6] Hursthouse argues that since virtue is, or crucially involves, practical wisdom – "the ability to reason correctly about practical matters" (1999: 154) – it must be puzzling why an agent should be good at reasoning well about some practical matters but not others. But it is not obvious why we should expect, for instance, that someone who is well aware of good reasons to help starving people will be equally able to see good reasons for being scrupulously veracious, or for restraining his jealousy of a sexual rival. (There is, besides, frequently room for dispute about what count as good reasons.) In a palpable hit, Rorty observes that the vaunted linkage of virtue and reason is more formulaic than helpful so long as it remains unaccompanied by any detailed prescriptions as to *how* our practical reasoning should be conducted (Rorty 1988: 308–9).

MERCUTIO

According to Aristotle, the big difference between the good man and the bad is that the former "tends to go right" and the latter to "go wrong" in regard to the three objects of choice – the noble, the advantageous and the pleasant – and their three contraries – the base, the injurious and the painful (Aristotle 1954: 33 [1105a]). Telling good agents from bad thus presupposes, on this account, that we are able to discriminate the positive objects from the negative. But this may not always be easy, as opinions may legitimately vary on what counts as noble, advantageous or pleasant; and further complications arise from the fact that noble, useful and pleasant ends may sometimes be in competition with one another. The difficulty persists of identifying the standards of practical reason that should govern the deliberations of the virtuous agent.

Agreeing on the standards can be difficult even for people who share the same cultural roots; in the case of those whose dominant cultural traditions differ, consensus may be perennially elusive. What people from one cultural background regard as admirably courageous behaviour may appear to those from another as pointless, foolhardy or morally repellent. The Crow warrior practice of touching an enemy with a "coup stick" (see Chapter 1, pp. 12–13) marked the acme of manly courage for the Crow, but probably looked like showy bravado to those members of neighbouring tribes who preferred their courage simple, not adorned. And a cultural tradition such as Japanese Bushido, which posits a glorious death in battle as the highest aspiration for a samurai, cuts little ice with most people from modern western democracies, who place a proportionately higher value on life than on martial honour. What, from a Bushido perspective, would count as honourable self-sacrifice on the battlefield might seem to the average American or Briton to be a profitless throwing of one's life away.

Even where alien paradigms of courage fail to engage us, it would be singularly ungracious to refuse to recognise something commendable in the behaviour they hold up for admiration. The fixing of the will in the face of adversity is morally admirable regardless of the moral status of the ends it serves. The Crow warrior who risked his life to touch an enemy with a coup stick aimed to obtain the enemy's recognition of his superior valour before striking him down. To defenders of more pacific philosophies, the warlike ideals of the Crow may appear provocative and vicious and the behaviour they inspire a parody of genuine courage. Yet to deny that the Crow manifested the moral excellence of courage seems not just wrong, but obviously wrong. If running up to an armed enemy and touching him with your coup stick isn't brave, then it's hard to know what is.

Wallace and Miller show us how we can, without inconsistency, admire a person's courage while deploring the uses to which he puts it. Courageous people can be troublemakers, as Rorty points out, because they look for opportunities to manifest their virtue (Rorty 1988: 300). Shakespeare's *Romeo and Juliet*, an everyday story of Renaissance Italian town folk, shows what happens when supporters of two powerful and fractious families are prepared to risk their own and other people's lives in a relentless contest in one-upmanship. Mercutio is a witty and whimsical, bold and loyal follower of the house of Montague, and Romeo's best friend. One hot day in Verona, when tempers are frayed and the "mad blood stirring," Mercutio and a small party of Montagues fall in with a band of Capulets led by the belligerent Tybalt, who is spoiling for a fight with Romeo. Mercutio is unwilling to forego a chance of antagonising his enemy:

> *Tybalt*: Gentlemen, good den; a word with one of you.
> *Mercutio*: And but one word with one of us? Couple it with something; make it a word and a blow.
> *Tybalt*: You shall find me apt enough to that, sir, an you will give me occasion.
> *Mercutio*: Could you not take some occasion without giving?
>
> (Act 3, sc.1, ll 37–42).

The arrival of Romeo at this point interrupts their growing quarrel. Tybalt immediately attempts to rile Romeo, calling him "boy" and "villain." But Romeo, who has recently been married in secret to Juliet, Tybalt's kinswoman, refuses to rise to the bait, declaring that he tenders the name of Capulet as dearly as his own. Romeo's apparently spineless acceptance of Tybalt's jibes rouses Mercutio's fury; if his friend will not take up the challenge, then he must do so himself.

Drawing his weapon, he compels Tybalt to cross swords with him.

Horror-struck, Romeo does his best to stop the fight. When words prove ineffective, he darts in between the combatants in an attempt to part them. But his well-meant intervention is disastrous, allowing Tybalt to thrust his sword beneath his arm and stab Mercutio fatally. While Tybalt and his companions quickly flee the scene, the dying Mercutio is carried to a nearby house, joking about his wound:

> *Mercutio*: No, 'tis not so deep as a well, nor so wide as a
> church door, but 'tis enough, 'twill serve. Ask for me to-
> morrow, and you shall find me a grave man.
>
> (ll. 93–96)

Shortly afterwards, the news of Mercutio's death is brought to the sorrowing Romeo:

> *Benvolio*: O Romeo, Romeo, brave Mercutio is dead!
> That gallant spirit hath aspir'd the clouds,
> Which too untimely here did scorn the earth.
>
> (ll. 113–15)

This pushes Romeo beyond the tipping point. Complaining that Juliet's beauty had made him effeminate, he rushes after Tybalt and, in a second furious duel, kills him.

Romeo's punishment for the slaying of Tybalt is to be permanently banished from Verona, on pain of death if he returns. The Prince, in delivering his sentence, does not mince his words: the mutual hatreds of the Montagues and Capulets have created a never-ending cycle of injury and retaliation. Pointless quarrels have brought needless, premature deaths; hot-blooded youth, egged on by the cooler enmities of age, has replaced order with anarchy. Yet in the public debate that follows the deaths of Mercutio and Tybalt, neither the Prince nor anyone else disputes the courage of the combatants. Mercutio is repeatedly referred to as "brave," and also as "gallant," "bold" and "stout," despite his having been a disturber of the public peace. At the very end of his life, Mercutio himself seems to grasp, too late, the error of his previous ways:

> *Mercutio*: . . . A plague o' both your houses!
> They have made worms' meat of me.
>
> (ll. 103–4)

Shakespeare's drama challenges medieval ideas about honour and allegiance which were still widely current (and doing harm) in the late sixteenth century. But it expresses no doubts that courage is compatible with fighting in a bad cause, and that a person can show genuine bravery in the pursuit of objectives that would be far better left alone. (Significantly, in the *First Part of King Henry IV* it is the cowardly knight Sir John Falstaff in whose mouth Shakespeare puts his most ironical critique of chivalric honour.) In seeing no antithesis between courage and morally defective objectives, Shakespeare displays moral intuitions in line with those of Wallace and Miller.

The colourful setting and stirring action of *Romeo and Juliet* and the iconic love story it tells can mask the repugnant bellicosity of several of the central characters, whose "pernicious rage," as the angry Prince observes, is too easily stirred up by "an airy word" (Act 1, sc. 1, ll. 82, 87). When Leonard Bernstein in *West Side Story* updated the plot to modern New York, the equally pugnacious behaviour of the Sharks and Jets seemed a good deal harder to condone, illustrating how familiarity can breed contempt. A real-life Mercutio who lived in our neighbourhood would be much less amusing and tolerable than one whose escapades were safely confined to the stage. Yet however little we might be prepared to countenance gang battles for dominance of the street, we ought still to be able to admire the Jets' and Sharks' readiness to face death and danger, and their strong group loyalties.

Praising a youthful gang member's courage may seem at odds with Plato's claim in Laches that courage and folly are inconsistent. A man who dives into deep water when he cannot swim, says Socrates, is not brave but merely stupid (Plato 1953a: 89 [193c]). But the disagreement (unlike the diver's water) is actually quite shallow. Suppose that, once the man has been fished out by the lifeguard, he is asked why he did such a foolish thing. If he answers, "For no reason, really; I just did it on a whim," he will earn no one's praise for courage. Nor will he do so if he offers a plainly ludicrous reason ("I was feeling bored," "I wanted to find out how deep the water was"). Compared with folly such as this, Mercutio's behaviour is as sensible as a dictionary. Like the Sharks and Jets, Mercutio serves a cause that, whatever its moral or prudential shortcomings, is backed by a certain conception of the good. Unlike the diver, Mercutio can cite something not wholly absurd that makes his risky action worth performing. The end of his life narrative follows coherently on what has gone before, even if it does betray a hint of second thoughts.

The same narrative coherence may also characterise the behaviour of the intrepid burglar or murderer, who takes a calculated risk to secure a valued, albeit immoral end. Even the youth of case (D) would have an intelligible reason for walking across the dangerous bridge if he wished to prove his fitness to join the Sharks; behaviour that is put down as mere showing off or bravado can have a serious purpose behind it. Denying courage to agents whose objectives we disapprove is a perennially tempting option, since a qualified condemnation can be easily confused with a partial approval. But if our own objectives include those of being truthful, gracious and tolerant, it is an option better reserved for cases where reason is entirely absent from the driving seat.

Six

COURAGE AS A GOAL, AND THE GOALS OF COURAGE

One of the minor ironies of the human condition is that where dangers do not exist, people often feel compelled to invent them. Thrill-seekers are commonly people whose lives, in their own estimation at least, are boring or unchallenging; they joyfully embrace carefully selected dangers as an antidote to dull monotony. But some thrill-seekers are looking for a subtler satisfaction: they want to prove to themselves or to others that they possess a courage which enhances their own value and sets them off from the crowd. Such an ambition might remind us of the heroes of history and legend, and of Aristotle's claim that the brave man is inspired by a conception of the noble. Yet it is arguably a somewhat meretricious courage that exists primarily to display its own charms. Here the normal order of things seems reversed: instead of courage being mustered in order to pursue an independently desirable object, a goal is sought, or manufactured, to serve as a pretext for courage. This is wanting to be brave for the sake of it, rather than for the sake of something else.

The result can still be genuine courage, though we may be reluctant to bestow much praise on it where the goal is selected merely for the degree of risk it involves. The person who does something dangerous solely to prove her courage at least has a reason for her action, unlike someone who puts herself in danger for no intelligible purpose. But if it is all one to her *how* she proves it, then she will deserve no more credit for volunteering to work with Médecins sans Frontières in a war-torn country than for taking up skydiving or potholing. The courage shown by Sophie Scholl would be less admirable if Sophie had been an indifferent anti-Nazi who simply wished to demonstrate her bravery. Courage is a praiseworthy quality in itself, but it is at its best only where it is summoned to serve morally fine ends for their own sake.

There is, however, a subtler form of motivation which is worth noting. Sometimes a person is committed to supporting a worthy but dangerous cause *and* keen to prove to himself or others that he has the necessary courage to do so. Such an agent wants to show that he has what it takes to be a servant of the noble, and not merely the kind of "guts" needed to be a skydiver or shark fisherman. His aspiration is not to be courageous *tout court*, but to be (e.g.) a courageous defender of his country, a brave opponent of political oppression or corruption in high places, or a silent, uncomplaining subject of illness or misfortune. The courage he aims at is, so to speak, not pure but applied. So summoning up the courage to ride a fast motorbike around a race track would not substitute for standing up to be counted when his religious beliefs or moral values were under threat, or his country's safety was at stake. Nor would such an agent readily switch from one objective to another, since his wish is to prove himself a brave servitor not of *any* noble cause but of some specific one. In fact, a person who claimed not to care what cause he served provided it was both worthy and dangerous could be accused of not really caring about virtue at all, but merely exploiting it for his own purposes.[1]

An agent who genuinely cares about a noble cause and aspires to the excellence of serving it bravely is not just *using* it for his own moral emolument. And courage will seem to him a valuable virtue *because* those who possess it are better servants of the good than those who lack it. Thus the enhanced self-esteem that he derives from acting bravely in a cause he believes in is intimately connected with his broader moral aspirations, and different from the mere pride in being courageous for courage's sake. Of course, a person may be mistaken about the goodness of the cause he is committed to, or the means to employ in pursuing it. But if, as was argued in the last chapter, we should be equally prepared to grant courage to people who fight on the right side of a conflict and the wrong, we should also allow that individual self-esteem can be legitimately enhanced by brave service even in a bad cause, provided that the agent *believes* it to be good.

What, though, if that cause should itself be that of demonstrating a "fitting" courage in the face of an enemy? Might we have been too brisk in dismissing as meretricious the demonstration of courage for its own sake? In a culture which believes that young men should aim to become brave soldiers or warriors, would those who rise to the challenge have just cause to celebrate, and expect others to celebrate, their courage? The answer, I think, is yes, because there is an important distinction between doing bold deeds because one wishes to impress oneself and others with one's courage, and doing them because one sees courageous action as an ethical ideal or moral duty.

These motives, however, are not mutually exclusive. Both are present in Henry Fleming, the "hero" of Stephen Crane's psychologically acute novella *The Red Badge of Courage*. Henry is a high-spirited farm lad who enlists in the Union Army during the American Civil War for a variety of reasons that include boredom, wanderlust and a somewhat unreflective patriotism; but, above all, Henry is moved by a fervent desire to realise a romantic ideal of himself as a man of courage. All his young life he had dreamed of battles, "of vague and bloody conflicts that had thrilled him with their sweep and fire." His only worry was that the war in his own country would be merely "a play affair," the merest echo of the glorious conflicts of the past. In lamenting modern degeneracy, Henry sounds almost like a rustic Nietzsche:

> He had long despaired of witnessing a Greeklike struggle. Such would be no more, he had said. Men were better, or more timid. Secular and religious education had effaced the throat-grappling instinct, or else firm finance held in check the passions.

(Crane 2008: 5)

But even if the present conflict fell short of the Homeric ideal, Henry thought, there would still be more glory in it than there could ever be in working on a farm.

On the eve of his first big battle, Henry's main fear is not that he might be wounded or killed, but that his courage might fail him at the critical moment, rendering him contemptible to his comrades and himself. While Henry is shrewd enough to doubt whether the seemingly confident men around him are really any braver than he is, the fluctuations of his own courage seem themselves so "many shameful crimes against the gods of traditions" (2008: 12). When the battle begins, Henry at first stands his ground well, and thinks himself a fine fellow for triumphing over "the red, formidable difficulties of war" (2008: 31). But his self-satisfaction is short-lived. When a charge by the enemy routs the Union troops, many of them, including Henry, flee for their lives. Later, after he has rallied his courage a little, he tries to stop some of his fellow soldiers from running away and receives a heavy blow on the head with a rifle butt from one of the panic-stricken fugitives.

When the dazed Henry rejoins his comrades, they mistakenly think that his "red badge of courage" has been received in honourable combat with the enemy. Ashamed to reveal the real truth, Henry determines to do something to be worthy of their new respect. Later in the battle he succeeds in keeping his head while his regiment defends a beleaguered position at a heavy cost in casualties. As the tide of battle turns, he and his comrades gradually begin to feel like men again (2008: 89). Finally Henry takes part in a daring counter-attack, helping to capture a Confederate flag and several prisoners. After the action, he and a fellow soldier sit down in some long grass:

> [Henry] nestled in it and rested, making a convenient rail support the flag. His friend, jubilant and glorified, holding his treasure with vanity, came to him there. They sat side by side and congratulated each other.
>
> (2008: 100)

Henry Fleming aspires to courage both because courage is for him an ethical ideal, and because he wants to impress those around him with his bravery so that, like his friend, he can feel proud of his achievement. These motives are not identical, but they are not incompatible or mutually undermining. If the first is morally superior, the second is morally acceptable so long as it does not prompt the agent to go looking for trouble. Yet, as Amélie Rorty reminds us, even those who cultivate courage as a high ethical ideal can be tempted to manufacture opportunities for courageous action. Plato, we have seen, strikes the right cautionary note: courage is a fine virtue, but it can easily get out of hand when not moderated by temperance (Plato 1953c: 528 [309e]).

MODERN COURAGE

Henry Fleming had no need to create the conditions for the exercise of courage; the Civil War conveniently provided them for him. A counterpart of Henry today might seek similar opportunities by joining NATO forces and going out to fight in Iraq or Afghanistan. Yet the scope for traditional applications of courage may seem to have narrowed for those of us who live in relatively stable, peaceful and affluent societies, who enjoy extensive democratic rights and personal liberties, and are cushioned against poverty, disease and ignorance. Pervasive health-and-safety legislation outlaws the taking of even minor risks, and we are protected from the normal shocks of life by the mothering attentions of the "nanny state." As Emma Restall Orr remarks, where government takes such good care of us, "there is no apparent need to find one's own strength" and no call for "true courage" (Orr 2007: 324). Courage can appear to be a significant virtue mostly for other, needier, people who lack our advantages – or a primarily "recreational" one to be practised in artificial situations of our own devising. Fortitude, too, may appear to have largely lost its point in an age abounding in literal and metaphorical anaesthetics. Why should we bother to endure what can readily be cured or compensated? It hardly takes fortitude (as distinct from a little patience) to face the typical minor irritations of everyday life: traffic jams, supermarket queues, spam emails, street litter, banal TV, obtrusive advertising and the like. Courage may seem to be a virtue that can be safely hung up in the moral wardrobe while the good weather lasts.

Of course, this is not really so. Courage is neither redundant nor outmoded although, as with any other virtue, its forms and applications need to adapt to the times. In many parts of the world, courage is needed as much as it ever was to resist or endure such perennial problems as injustice, oppression, social upheaval, ethnic tensions, poverty, endemic sickness, famine and urban blight. When Nelson Mandela and the ANC sounded the cry of freedom and forced an end to apartheid in South Africa, they joined a long and honourable line of those who have struggled courageously in the cause of the enslaved and the downtrodden. And almost every day one hears some new story of moral and physical courage from such international trouble spots as Burma, Darfur, Tibet, Pakistan and the Near and Middle East.

Although life in the modern developed world may, on the whole, offer fewer dangers of violent death at the hands of an enemy,[2] political oppression, hunger or disease, it has become notoriously frenetic, stressful, highly competitive, socially fluid and, for many individuals, very lonely. The concrete jungle can be quite as intimidating as a real jungle. Traditional sources of support and anchors of personal identity such as the nuclear family, the church or the local community are no longer as robust as they once were, and are not available to everyone. The mass immigration experienced by many western countries, while it may enhance cultural diversity, can also bring social instability, a decline in the sense of neighbourhood and a sense of "not belonging." In the century since Nietzsche's fool proclaimed the death of God, the loss by many people of religious faith has necessitated painful adjustments to their spiritual and ethical outlooks.

Courage is just as much needed to face feelings of doubt, alienation, isolation or hopelessness as it is to meet an enemy on the battlefield.

Jonathan Lear's study of the Crow Indians offers an instructive example of how changing situations require different forms of courage. When land-hungry white settlers moved into their territory and gradually expropriated more and more of their traditional hunting grounds, the Crow, under the wise leadership of their chief Plenty Coups, saved what they could from the ruins by adopting a painful policy of cautious cooperation with the US government. Faced with the choice of "adapt or die," they came to see that the bravery of the warrior is not the only possible sort of courage. Another kind involves the willingness to abandon cherished but no longer workable ways of life and embrace new ones, with all their accompanying risks and uncertainties. To preserve what they could of their land, the Crow turned from hunting to farming, and became obedient citizens of the USA.

Not the least risk of such a strategy is that it is open to serious misconstruction, even by its own adherents: adaptability can appear a lack of steadfastness and the readiness to cooperate be confused with surrender. The trouble with adopting a radical solution to a problem is that it is hard to be sure that one is doing the right thing, practically or morally. Yet clawing to keep hold of an untenable position (or of one's illusions) may show one to be not so much steadfast as rash. As Plenty Coups later explained, the decision to engage with the white man rather than continue a futile opposition had been taken "because we plainly saw that this course was the only one which might save our beautiful country for us" (Lear 2006: 143).

At the beginning of the twenty-first century, it is not just a single country that is in need of saving but the whole world. The twin dangers of anthropogenic global warming and the gross overexploitation of natural resources are now generally acknowledged by the scientific community, though estimates vary concerning both the scale and the timeline of the developing crisis. But even the most optimistic estimates concede that the earth cannot in the long term sustain the pressures put on it by an ever-growing population avid to share in the energy-costly lifestyle currently enjoyed by the citizens of developed countries. Unless carbon emissions into the atmosphere can be substantially reduced below present levels, global temperatures will continue to rise, causing profound changes to weather patterns and catastrophic rises in sea levels with the melting of the Antarctic and Greenland ice caps. Effective international consensus on how to deal with the crisis has so far proved depressingly elusive, and rapidly industrialising countries such as China are understandably reluctant to restrain their development while the developed nations refuse to countenance any meaningful reductions in their own energy use.

In part, the difficulty of achieving workable international agreements to avert global ecological catastrophe rests on the entrapment of energy-hungry nations in the predicament known to game theorists as a "prisoner's dilemma." Briefly, this means that countries that would be willing to limit their own carbon emissions (at considerable cost to their economies) if other countries would do the same, fear that if they honour an agreement to make cuts while others default on their commitments, the defaulting nations will benefit from their own sacrifices without having to make any of their own. To lessen the risks of cheating, robust enforcement agencies are needed that could compel nation states to maintain their international agreements; but the prospect of such agencies at the moment appears slim.

A similar dilemma confronts industrial companies and private individuals, who are likewise wary of incurring the risks and expenses of switching to a less carbon-costly regimen unless they can be assured that others will do the same. To run the risks even while this assurance is lacking, or where it is probable that others will not follow suit, takes considerable courage. It is hard to abandon the familiar and embark on a new and uncertain course of life or action, especially where one fears that others might take advantage of one's self-denial. Sadly but unsurprisingly, few political leaders with an eye to the next election, or anxious company directors with shareholders to satisfy, have found the courage to commit their countries or corporations to remotely adequate action to restrict carbon emissions. It requires far less courage to talk than to act, and to promise (literally) the earth while doing next to nothing to make the promise good.

It is not only courage that is needed if looming climatic and ecological disasters are to be averted; all the cardinal virtues are. *Prudence* dictates that humanity should take appropriate action before it is too late to prevent runaway climate change. *Temperance* is the virtue to cultivate if we are to live a less environmentally demanding lifestyle, reducing our luxuries (as well as what we misrepresent to be necessities). *Justice* is required to achieve an equitable distribution of burdens and benefits, and to ensure that the neediest members of the human community do not pay the lion's share of the cost of others' extravagance. All four virtues, and not just courage, are the hinges on which our common future hangs.[3]

WHISTLE-BLOWING

One striking example of how courage adapts to the times is afforded by the modern phenomenon of "whistle-blowing": a term denoting the public disclosure by employees or members of organisations (or sometimes well-informed outsiders) of misdemeanours committed by, or on behalf of, the company or other body. Like a referee of a football match who spots a foul, whistle-blowers aim to stop the illegal action in its tracks and ensure that the game is played by the proper rules. In the UK and several other countries a measure of legal protection is now available to those who in the public interest "blow the whistle" about wrongdoing. The UK *Public Interest Disclosure Act 1998* protects company workers who have a reasonable belief that they are disclosing (among other things) a criminal offence, the breach of a legal obligation, an undue risk posed to the health or safety of an individual, or damage to the environment. Yet in spite of the safeguards laid down in law, whistle-blowers often run serious risks when they publicly reveal that a company or some other collective body has been acting badly.

In an article on whistle-blowing in academic medicine, R. Rhodes and J. J. Strain paint a black picture of the fate of faculty, students and technical staff who report concerns about ethical problems relating to research:

> Whistleblowers are ostracised, pressured to drop allegations, and threatened with counterallegations. They lose desirable assignments, have their research support reduced and their promotions and raises denied. Their contracts are not renewed, and they are fired. Whistleblowers are obvious targets, especially in a time of financial cutbacks, re-engineering and downsizing, and everyone knows it.
> (Rhodes and Strain 2004: 35)

Other writers point out that the "payback" for whistle-blowing can extend far beyond the workplace. According to T. Faunce, S. Bolsin and W.-P. Chan, "[u]nemployment, bankruptcy, litigation, divorce, mental illness, and suicide are common outcomes of the act of whistleblowing" (Faunce et al. 2004: 42).

It would be wrong to think that whistle-blowing, with its attendant dangers, is confined to white-collar or professional working environments; for poor ethical practice is encountered on the factory floor just as often as in the board or committee room. Whistle-blowing always calls for the moral courage to risk ostracism, unpopularity with colleagues, bosses and other superiors, and the setting of an invisible ceiling to one's career prospects. It can also require the courage to face severe material hardship where the consequences of revealing an unpalatable truth are loss of employment, poverty, breakdown of family relationships, or mental illness.

Whistle-blowing typically pits a relatively powerless and isolated individual against a powerful company or institution. Yet, as in the original contest of David and Goliath, victory does not always go to the larger contender. It did not, for instance, when the American geochemist Clair Patterson campaigned to convince the world and the US government that the Ethyl Corporation and other manufacturers of lead additives in gasoline were taking quite unjustifiable risks with public health. Tetraethyl lead (TEL) was first added to gasoline as an anti-knock agent in the early 1920s and from the outset was a source of concern to many who believed it rash to release large quantities of this highly toxic substance into the atmosphere. But the producers of TEL moved quickly to allay alarm by recruiting their own "experts" to testify that the use of TEL raised the levels of atmospheric lead only slightly above normal background levels and posed no significant risk to human health. The industry's key authority was the occupational physician Dr Robert Arthur Kehoe, who bullishly challenged critics to "show me the data" on the actual harmful effects of lead additives and argued that it was folly to cripple a profitable industry on the basis of purely speculative worries. Strongly supported (and financed) by the lead and motor-manufacturing industries, Kehoe rapidly obtained academic chairs and distinctions in the field of public health, plus the lucrative post of Medical Director of the Ethyl Corporation.

In the four following decades, virtually no systematic independent research was done on the health and environmental effects of atmospheric lead, and national governments were mostly content to accept the bland assurances of the manufacturers that the risks, if any, were minimal. Not until the 1960s did the sceptics find a champion with the knowledge and the courage to take on the Ethyl Corporation, challenge the complacency engendered by the "Kehoe paradigm" ("show me the data"), and reveal the real harm being done by the use of TEL.

Clair Patterson (1922–95) was already a scientist of considerable note when he turned his attention to the problem of atmospheric lead pollution. He had made his name in the 1950s by determining with unprecedented precision the true age of the earth (4.55 billion, plus or minus 70 million years) from the scrupulously careful measurement of microgram quantities of lead in rocks and the analysis of their isotopic composition. Patterson was just the man to establish exactly how much of the lead in the environment was natural and how much was contributed by human activities. With characteristic care and thoroughness he embarked on a series of experiments designed to compare past and present lead levels. By measuring the amount of lead contained in Greenland ice cores of different ages, in ancient and modern skeletons, and in the bones and tissues of deep-sea fishes, by 1965 Patterson could announce that a pre-industrial atmospheric lead concentration of 0.0005 micrograms per cubic metre had risen to more than 1 microgram per cubic metre in urban environments – a massive 2,000-fold increase (Nriagu 1998: 77). He also showed that the harmful effects of ingesting lead at low concentrations were not of a kind to manifest themselves quickly, and that by the time the sort of data that Kehoe demanded became available, the health of millions worldwide would have been irreparably damaged.

Patterson's unremitting efforts to get the lead out of gasoline continued in the face of every kind of opposition and harassment from the additives industry. It was not until 1986 that TEL was finally banned in US gasoline. Bill Bryson lists some of the obstacles that Patterson encountered in the course of his "hellish campaign":

> Ethyl was a powerful global corporation with many friends in high places. . . . Patterson suddenly found research funding withdrawn or difficult to acquire. The American Petroleum Institute cancelled a research contract with him, as did the United States Public Health Service, a supposedly neutral body.
>
> (Bryson 2004: 203)

The trustees of Patterson's own institute, Caltech, were pressured by industry representatives to sack him, and Ethyl allegedly offered to endow a chair at Caltech on condition that Patterson be dismissed. He was also pointedly passed over when appointments were made to influential federally funded investigative panels (Bryson 2004: 203–4).

Patterson's fight to eliminate lead additives, waged at great personal cost, finally achieved its goal when the USA and other countries legislated to make the use of TEL illegal. Herbert Needleman, remarking that Patterson – that "immoveable man" – "was the primary scientific force in altering the narrow world view of lead toxicity," pays him a well-deserved tribute: "The blood levels of today's children are a testimony to his brilliance and integrity" (Needleman 1998: 85). David brings down Goliath with a well-aimed stone; but the outcome could so easily have been different, and would have been if Patterson had lacked the courage to take on some of the most powerful vested interests in America.

COURAGE AND THE LOSS OF MEANING

" 'How much truth can a spirit *endure?*'," wrote Nietzsche in 1888; " 'how much truth does a spirit *dare?*' – this became for me the real standard of value" (Nietzsche 1968: 536). For Nietzsche, the truth to be confronted was that the world was not a repository of objective values but a blank slate on which human beings inscribe the values they will. This is a frightening, even shocking truth, and it takes courage to recognise that the only norm is normlessness. What Nietzsche calls "the most fundamental nihilism" denies that there are any values "out there" to help us to write the narratives of our lives. No God is the author of our being or the giver of our laws. The world itself is not the subject of any teleological narrative, and nothing it contains, including ourselves, has been put there for any purpose. To grasp these truths is to move beyond good and evil as traditionally conceived, into a new spiritual environment in which values have to be constructed *de novo*, while also being clearly recognised *as* constructions. But for many people who glimpse the truth, the dissolution of the old metaphysical and moral certainties is too awful to be contemplated; and since they cannot abide the realisation that the world is objectively valueless, they either self-deceptively cling on to the old beliefs or find others to put in their place. In the pathetic attempt to exchange old lamps for new, scoffs Nietzsche, supposedly advanced thinkers have lighted on such illusory universal ideals as democracy, the greatest happiness of the greatest number, social progress, and the objectivity of science.

For Nietzsche, such evasion is not only cowardly but represents a lost creative opportunity. What average human beings regard as a comforting supportive framework, "higher beings" see as an imprisoning cage of old, tired meanings which have to be rejected before the elevation of man can take place (1968: 537). "Higher beings" (aka "the stronger sort of men") show their courage first by dismissing illusions and accepting "the world as it is, without subtraction, exception, or selection" (1968: 537), second by resolutely constructing new meanings which lay no bogus claims to objectivity of the kind craved by the "herd."

Nietzsche's contention that it takes courage to face the prospect of a universe which is purposeless and without moral pointers has been repeated by many later writers, who see what Tillich refers to as "the anxiety of emptiness" as a leitmotif of the contemporary human condition (Tillich 2000: 47). Tillich notes that there are many things to which people were once passionately devoted but whose day is now done. The difficulty is to know what to put in their place, and nothing quite seems to fit the bill:

> Everything is tried and nothing satisfies. The contents of the tradition, however excellent, however praised, however loved once, lose their power to give content *today*. And present culture is even less able to provide the content.
>
> (2000: 48)

The main reason that nothing satisfies is that identified by Nietzsche: we have lost faith in God or an absolute moral law to provide us with fixed reference points. While modern man still hankers for a "spiritual centre," he no longer believes in its possibility. There thus seems to be no escape from our predicament; "[t]he anxiety of emptiness drives us to the abyss of meaninglessness" (Tillich 2000: 48). For Tillich, this situation reveals at once both the necessity and the difficulty of mustering "the courage to be" – that is, the courage to be self-affirming, self-respecting, purposeful individuals, maintaining a sense of value (or what we earlier called a conception of the good) in a world in which nothing objectively matters.

Heidegger similarly spoke of the courage needed to live in a world which provides no external standards of right and wrong and in which we must devise, rather than discover, a purpose for living. In *Being and Time* he emphasises the anxiety we feel as a result of our finitude and our "being-towards-death" – that is, our sense of ourselves as frail and transient creatures who live amidst a welter of conflicting meanings in the dispiriting awareness that we may die at any time. Heidegger recommends that we should face our predicament with the resolution (*Entschlossenheit*) to be self-directing individuals, avoiding what he terms "lostness in the 'they' " of other people, and making our own decisions on how to "be in the world" (Heidegger 1962: 344–5).

From an early-twenty-first century perspective, it may appear that earlier reports of the death of meaning have been much exaggerated. The rapid social, technological and economic changes of the twentieth century, coupled with its terrible wars, genocides and ideological conflicts, were enough to give even the least reflective individual a sense of being lost in a senseless and indifferent universe. Yet if our contemporary world is scarcely a less conflicted one than that of fifty or a hundred years ago, it seems less characteristic of the *Zeitgeist* to complain that existence is empty of meaning and all our acts objectively pointless. The leitmotif of a world that had drifted away from its existential moorings, expressed not only in philosophical texts of the period but also in such literary works as T. S. Eliot's poem *The Waste Land* (1922), is not so prominent in our own postcolonial, multicultural environment, which is perforce more concerned with problems arising from competition among values than with the loss of values.

Generally speaking, traditional religious and ethical outlooks have shown more resilience in an otherwise changing world than many early twentieth-century prophets predicted. And while more people than formerly are prepared to take a liberal, live-and-let-live approach to alternative world views which are prepared to return the courtesy, sadly bigotry, intolerance and missionary zeal to convert others to the "right" ways of thinking and acting are not yet consigned to the dustbin of history. Too much conviction, rather than too little, is responsible for many of the conflicts of the present day. Maybe Nietzsche was right that we live in a world with no determinate moral structure and offering no objective pointers to meaningful existence. But if he was, then there are many people who are still to get the message.

Still, it undeniably takes courage to find our feet again when some of our fundamental assumptions have disappeared from under them. Where the narrative of one's life has pivoted on one's relationship to a divine being, the onset of disbelief plainly necessitates a major rewriting of the plot line. This can be a painful exercise even for those who otherwise welcome the freedom that disbelief brings. The loss of religious belief can also be particularly painful where it alienates a person from those he loves and who love him, or puts him at odds with other members of his community; someone in this predicament may need the courage to face losing not only his God but his friends and family too.

DOUBT, CERTAINTY AND TOLERANCE

It is usually taken for granted that certainty is comforting and doubt disturbing, and religious believers are accordingly apt to pity non-believers for their lack of a secure spiritual anchorage. Yet certainty can be quite as uncomfortable to live with as uncertainty, and provide an equally great test of courage. In times when God was seen rather as a vengeful judge than a loving father, and fear of the Lord the constant refrain of teachers and preachers, religious melancholia was a widespread phenomenon. People of all social ranks and educational levels worried about their souls and feared the wrath of a God who knew the precise tally of their actions. This was small wonder when the fate of sinners was thought to be never-ending punishment in a place of almost unimaginable suffering. Even the stoutest-hearted could be terrified by descriptions such as the following, from a fourteenth-century writer, of the punishment in store for most human beings after death:

O how great will be the pains of the damned who remain
without remission eternally in wretchedness, knowing neither
peace nor rest! . . . For incomparable pain is there,
inextinguishable fire, worms which cannot be killed;
intolerable stenches, darkness which can be touched, the
dreadful appearance of wicked demons, the shame of sin,
and despair of ever receiving any assistance or any good
thing.

(van Vliederhoven 2008: 10)

To avoid giving way to terminal despair if one believed such horrors must have taken enormous resolution. And many people firmly believed them, not only in the earlier centuries of Christianity but well into modern times.[4] Particularly dispiriting has been the Calvinist doctrine of predestination, which holds that salvation or damnation depends entirely on God's gratuitous election, with the implication that even a morally virtuous person may still be damned. Living with the belief that nothing that one does will make the slightest difference to whether one is saved or damned must stretch the most self-possessed person's fortitude to the limit.

Of course, not all certainties have been as disturbing as some of the traditional Christian ones. But the moral of the example is that we cannot simply equate conviction with ease and doubt with unease and associate the need for courage exclusively with the latter. Admittedly, being in a state of uncertainty is apt to be unsettling, and it can take courage to resist the temptation to sweep doubts under the carpet. Doubts have a natural dynamic that certainties lack; they press to be resolved, and trouble us until they are. However, it does not follow that we always feel more comfortable with the answers we find.

It can take additional fortitude to bear our own uncertainties when others flaunt their certainties before us. "The best lack all conviction," wrote W. B. Yeats in 1921, "while the worst / Are full of passionate intensity" (Yeats 1950: 211). He might well have said the same thing in the aftermath of 9/11. People who are too sure of themselves and the merits of their own cause have been prominent on both sides of the ideological divide which has opened up between the west and militant Islam in recent years. Those who are full of passionate intensity have liked to portray as weak, half-hearted, even traitorous any who have dared to suggest that the issues might not be quite as black and white as the zealots maintain. To be a moderate, sceptical voice in the context of the "war against terror" has required, even in Washington or London, considerable moral courage in view of the official disapproval of such a stance; in some places it has called for physical courage too.

If passionate intensity in the service of bad causes is the source of much harm, there is a difference between looking carefully before we leap and merely sitting on the fence while things happen around us. Yeats was not *praising* "the best" for their lack of convictions. There is nothing courageous about refusing to commit to any causes for fear of making mistakes. That is the fault for which the writer of the Book of Revelation criticised the Laodiceans, who were said to be ever "lukewarm, and neither hot nor cold" (Rev. 3:16). From a Nietzschean perspective too, discarding the illusions of the "herd" is not the end point of moral and intellectual endeavour, but the essential preliminary to a creative reconstruction of values.[5]

To live in a world of uncertainty and clashing opinions requires a courage consisting of three intertwined strands. First, we need the courage to pursue causes even though we know they may turn out to be wrong. Second, we must be brave enough to refuse the siren attractions of dogmatism and actively expose our ideas to external challenges, allowing them the chance to prove their relative worth or worthlessness. Third, we require the courage to live with difference, peaceably (which does not mean complacently) in a world where conceptions of the good vary markedly and disconcertingly. This is the courage to pursue our own course and express our own opinions even when they are idiosyncratic or unpopular, and to tolerate the same in others even where their words or actions disturb us.

There is nothing very novel about these claims; John Stuart Mill stated something very like them in *On Liberty* (1910 [1859]). In mid-nineteenth-century Britain, people were no longer put to death for holding unorthodox views but sanctions were still inflicted on those who refused to toe the conventional line on morality, politics or religion. "Our merely social intolerance," Mill wrote, "kills no one, roots out no opinions, but induces men to disguise them, or to abstain from any active effort for their diffusion" (Mill 1910: 93). To avoid public disfavour required being "conformers to common-place, or time-servers for truth." The suppression of individuality in thought or action created a desert and called it peace: "the price paid for this sort of intellectual pacification is the sacrifice of the entire moral courage of the human mind" (1910: 93).

Such moral courage, though, should not, Mill thought, take the guise of a stubborn refusal to entertain the possibility that we might be wrong, or an unwillingness to put our own ideas to the test. It should rather be the courage to live with uncertainty, where we treat our opinions as working hypotheses and not unassailable dogmas:

> Complete liberty of contradicting and disproving our opinion
> is the very condition which justifies our assuming its truth for
> purposes of action; and on no other terms can a being with
> human faculties have any rational assurance of being right.
>
> (1910: 81)

Refusing to let our beliefs be challenged has another down-side too: in time they lose their vitality and command only "a dull and torpid assent," failing any longer to stimulate our intelligence or engage our imagination. At that point they may still serve "to pelt adversaries with" but they have lost their power over the mind (1910: 100–1). The heavy penalty for those guilty of intellectual cowardice is intellectual stagnation.

ENVOI

Arrived at the end of our study of courage, we have seen no reason to suppose courage to be an outdated or redundant virtue. *Plus ça change, plus c'est la même chose*: the forms and contexts of courage may be specific to an age, but the virtue itself is a perennial requisite for individual and social flourishing. Courage is a virtue which finite and vulnerable human beings cannot do without. Now, as ever, we need courage because there is so much that can go wrong for us. Courage, whether public and dramatic or private and personal, retains a seat at the top table of virtues.

Would it have been better if human beings had lived in an earthly paradise from which all pain, suffering, illness, disappointment, loss and even death itself were absent? In such an environment the need for courage would be lacking, since there would never be anything to threaten or frighten us. Yet it is not clear that we would be better off in a world which offered us no opportunities to exercise strength of will and "screw our courage to the sticking place." Certainly there would be less for us to admire in people who never had occasion to show courage. If courage is noble, as Aristotle claimed, then we should feel only a muted regret that our world is not a paradise. But this does not mean that we should go out of our way to create opportunities for bravery; that would be flying in the face of that other cardinal virtue of prudence. Most people's lives provide them with plenty of openings for courage, without their having to seek them.

In George Herbert's poem *Constancie*, the "honest man" is one

> Who, when great trials come,
> Nor seeks, nor shuns them; but doth calmly stay,
> Till he the thing and the example weigh;
> All being brought into a summe,
> What place or person calls for, he doth pay.
>
> (Herbert 1961: 63)

Herbert's is as good a thumbnail portrayal of courage as any we have met, and there is nothing outmoded about the ideal he presents. This is the courage to face what Stephen Crane has called "the unutterable midnights of the universe" as well as the lesser twilit moments of daily life (Crane 2008: 233). When troubles come, courage may prove our saving grace, in more senses than one.

Notes

ONE LOCATING COURAGE

1 Sometimes we speak of bravery where talk of courage might seem rather high-flown. E.g. we prefer to describe someone as "brave" in the dentist's chair rather than "courageous." But this is not because we think that the dental patient displays some quality that is different from courage. It is rather that English idiom favours the use of "brave" to characterise behaviour which is at the lower end of the spectrum of courageous behaviour (though the word "brave" is not restricted to that).

2 One might wonder, incidentally, whether the story Aristotle tells must also require another quality in the virtue-seeker, namely the resoluteness to see the process through. But if so this is problematic, since it now looks as though we need to have a virtue before we can acquire virtue, thus raising the question how this virtue (itself a species, or close relative, of courage) is supposed to be acquired – for until we have resoluteness, we cannot apply that quality in its own acquisition, while once we have it we no longer need to acquire it. It is not clear what answer an Aristotelian could consistently give to this.

3 Two remarks about women's courage that give the flavour of Aristotle's view are to be found in the Politics: "the courage of a man is shown in commanding, of a woman in obeying," and "[f]or a man would be thought a coward if he had no more courage than a courageous woman" (Aristotle 1905: 51, 109 [1260a, 1277b]). For more on the (mainly unflattering) views of female courage held in classical Greece, see below, Chapter 3.

4 One Vietnam veteran is quoted by John McCain as describing bravery on the battlefield as "impossible to comprehend, really, even if you witness it . . . It's one mad moment." Later McCain remarks that

"They don't give Medals of Honor for rational acts of courage" (McCain 2004: 198).

5   But don't thrill-seekers and show-offs enjoy the sensation of fear when they put themselves at risk? Probably not. It is more likely that they take pleasure in being noticed or admired, or improving their status among their peers, or proving their skill, or demonstrating their virility. (For more on the psychology of fear and courage, see Chapter 3.)

6   For an overview of the literature, see Christina Saltaris (2002); also G. Kochanska (1991), D. T. Lykken (1982).

7   Late in the opera, Siegfried does claim to have discovered what fear is, when he looks upon a woman for the first time (the Valkyrie Brünnhilde in her enchanted sleep). Amazed and disconcerted by her beauty, the hero exclaims: "That is no man! Burning bewitchment pierces my heart! Fiery pangs rivet my eyesight" (Wagner 1960: 33). Siegfried's astonished reaction, however, is much more accurately designated sex shock than fear.

8   Interestingly, there are some apparent precedents for this mode of speech in Plato and Aristotle. See Aristotle (1954: 64 [1115a]; Plato 1953b: 375, 386–7 [218, 230–31]).

9   Since Kennedy wrote his book, two other well-known political figures have produced studies of courageous people: British Prime Minister Gordon Brown, whose *Courage: Eight Portraits* appeared in 2007, and US Presidential candidate John McCain, who published his *Why Courage Matters* in 2004. Whether or not it takes courage to be a politician, politicians appear to be fascinated by courage.

TWO   THE REALITY OF COURAGE

1   As we have seen in Chapter 1, Aristotle thought that *acts* could sometimes count as courageous even when the agent performing them could not be ascribed the corresponding virtue. In a formulation suggested to me by an anonymous referee, Aristotle's view is that an act is courageous "if and only if it is the sort of act that a courageous person acting in character would perform in that situation" (an anonymous referee). While this distinguishes such acts from those merely bold or daring ones which a virtuously courageous person would be unlikely to perform, their precise status remains puzzling, since it is unclear what kinds

of alternative rational sanction they might have which would ensure that they include only such as a truly courageous agent would perform.

2 I am indebted to an anonymous reader for the publisher for some of the formulations of ideas in this paragraph.

3 Significantly, the word "courage" does not even have an entry in the Index to their book.

4 Staub, in an interesting anticipation of more recent discussions of the bearing of situation on moral motivation (see note 5 below), usefully lists nine "aspects of situations" that can influence whether people produce helpful behaviour or not. These include how clear-cut the need for helpful intervention is, the magnitude of need ("usually, the greater the need, the more help will follow"), the extent to which responsibility for helping is diffused among a number of people, and the costs of helping (in effort, time, energy, material goods and risk to oneself) (1978–9: Vol. 2, 9–10).

5 While the Polish woman undoubtedly displayed courage, is it also appropriate to ascribe to her the *ethike arete* of courage? Not, I suggest, if the act in question was a "one-off," an exceptional piece of behaviour which she failed to replicate in other similar circumstances. Contemporary sceptics about virtue such as John Doris and Gilbert Harman, drawing on empirical psychological research, have cast doubt on the existence of general character traits of the kind envisaged by Aristotle in his account of the moral virtues and vices, arguing that the actual behaviour of individuals shows much less consistency, and far more situational plasticity, than most previous theorists and moralists have supposed (see Doris 2002; Harman 1999–2000). As the jury is still out on these highly controversial claims, I shall not discuss them here. But it may be noted that even Doris concedes that people often exhibit a fair degree of consistency when acting within certain more specific kinds of context (e.g. in Doris 2005: 667f.). This is borne out in the Oliners' ability to distinguish between those who normally helped Jews and those who refused. Yet one can imagine a person who helped Jews but could not "summon up the courage" to help people of another ethnic or religious group with whom she found it harder to empathise. On this evidence, we might be hesitant about ascribing to her the *ethike arete* of courage, even disregarding any broader doubts we might have about the reality of general traits of character. Aristotle maintains that

virtuous acts (those which manifest genuine *ethike arete*) "must proceed from a firm and unchangeable character," a conception which situationists who dispute the existence of fixed characters must reject (1954: 34 [1105a]). But most people would presumably agree that if there are moral virtues, then subjects who have them can be expected to manifest them in a reasonably consistent and regular fashion, not merely at whim or in narrowly defined circumstances only.

6   I am indebted for this suggestion to Tim Chappell.

7   That there exist any virtues of this description is, however, disputed by situationists such as Doris. See note 5 above.

THREE   CARDINAL VIRTUE OR MACHO VICE?

1   The alternative Latin term *fortitudo* is less explicitly gendered but for some writers of classical Latin meant primarily military courage and so by implication the courage of men; though others, including Cicero, granted that it could be significantly displayed in domestic situations too.

2   Conceivably Aristotle might have allowed that a female *warrior* (e.g. one of the legendary Amazons) could be courageous. If so, then it would be more correct to describe Aristotle as believing courage to be a virtue involved in characteristically male activities than as holding it to be an exclusively male virtue. This would still not have allowed for many – if any – actual women of Aristotle's own society to qualify as courageous on his measure.

3   It should not be assumed that the words attributed to Pericles were precisely those spoken by him; probably Thucydides is giving us an imaginative reconstruction of the address based on eyewitness accounts. Nevertheless, as one recent editor has written, "the speech is a most eloquent defence of the virtues of the Athenian way of life in the 5th century BC" (Chris Scarre, in Thucydides 1994: 95n35).

4   The standard life of Mary Macarthur is by Mary Agnes Hamilton (1925). For a brief but vivid account of Mary's activities in the pre-war years, see Juliet Nicolson (2006: 200, 203–5).

5   The *locus classicus* is Robert L. Trivers (1971). For a very readable summary of the literature on the evolution of morality, see Matt Ridley (1997).

6   The sense in which cardinal virtues are "constitutive conditions" of all virtues is more fully articulated in Oderberg (1999: 316).

1 "Fortitude" is further disadvantaged by having no snappy adjectival form. The adjective "fortitudinous" is to be found in the dictionary but very rarely outside it.

2 The close connection between fortitude and patience was also spotlighted by the poet John Dryden, who remarked that "the Fortitude of a Christian consists in Patience, and Suffering for the Love of GOD, whatever Hardships can befall in the World; not in any great Attempt, or in performance of those Enterprises which the poets call Heroique"; though Dryden did concede that generals, monarchs and magistrates will also need to practise an "active Fortitude" (along with "coercive Power" and "awful Command") (Dryden 1697: xv).

3 Sometimes what appears at first to be virtuous fortitude may be instead the morally more neutral trait of stubbornness. Immovability can, in fact, have a variety of other grounds besides fortitude and obstinacy, including inertia, laziness or accidie. We should beware of ascribing fortitude too quickly to people who exhibit seeming firmness in dangerous or painful situations; we need to establish that they are standing fast and not merely stuck fast.

4 Appropriately, the Latin word *robur* means both strength and a particularly hard species of oak.

5 Franciszek Gajowniczek, whose place Maximilan Kolbe took, was chiefly worried that his death would leave his wife and family without protection; in the event, he, but not they, survived the camp. Kolbe was subsequently canonised by Pope John Paul II in 1982, who described him as "the patron saint of our difficult century."

6 Would patience of the most perfect variety consist in not having the disturbing feelings in the first place? No, because that would not be patience but the far less desirable condition of insensibility.

7 In fairness, it should be added that Marcus Aurelius did not hold that we should concentrate solely on taking care of the self and let the world go hang. The virtuous Stoic does not shirk whatever duties his station of life imposes on him, whether he is a slave or an emperor; nevertheless, when things get tough he can always find a bolt-hole in what Isaiah Berlin has memorably called "the inner citadel" of the self (see Berlin 1969).

8 For a fascinating discussion of the impact of Epictetus' brand of

stoicism on American forces personnel, some of whom have carried his *Enchiridion* into the battle zone along with the Bible, see N. Sherman 2005: *passim*.

9 According to a poll taken in Britain a few years ago, "If" is the nation's favourite poem. Readers may like to consider what this says about the character of contemporary Britain and its literary tastes.

10 Note that not all martyrs, Christian or otherwise, have treated death as if it were unimportant. Many have regarded it as a terrible thing to die but still the best option in the circumstances. (As Tim Chappell has pointed out to me, this is one particularly admirable paradigm of courage.)

11 Canus's mode of dying bears a striking similarity to that of the disgraced Thane of Cawdor described in Shakespeare's *Macbeth*: ". . . nothing in his life / Became him like the leaving it: he died / As one that had been studied in his death / To throw away the dearest thing he ow'd / As 'twere a careless trifle" (*Macbeth*, Act I, sc, 4, ll. 7–11).

12 According to Kai Nielsen, Austin, a prominent Oxford philosopher of the mid-twentieth century, expressed his dislike of "singing songs" at a time when he knew he was dying of cancer. See Nielsen 2000: 154.

FIVE   COURAGE AND GOODNESS

1 Aristotle might have conceded the spiritedness (*thumos*) of her behaviour, but he would not have identified such *thumos* with virtuous courage, given the internal connection between courage and the good.

2 This case is suggested by a scene in the movie *The Godfather: Part II*. In the film version, the assassin, having at immense personal risk succeeded in killing his victim in a crowded airport, is himself shot dead by police immediately afterwards.

3 Von Wright's words are reminiscent of the statement of the nineteenth-century observer of London low life, Henry Mayhew, that "[t]he expert burglar is generally very ingenious in his devices, and combines manual dexterity with courage" (Mayhew 1987: 249). Two hundred years earlier an Elizabethan parson had sounded a similar note in a sermon: "First, fortitude and stoutness of courage and also boldness of mind, is commended of some men to be a virtue; which being granted who is it then that will not judge thieves to be virtuous? For they be of all men most stout and hardy and most without fear" (quoted in Salgado 1977: 134).

4   It may be worthwhile to remind the reader here that in this book I am using the word "brave" as a synonym of "courageous" rather than of "bold" or "daring"; it thus carries the same moral resonances as the term "courageous." This employment of "brave" may appear slightly arbitrary to some, but it is sanctioned, I believe, by popular usage.

5   Hursthouse gives the example of the puzzlement we would feel if we found that someone we thought to be charitable or honest had performed a cruel or dishonest act (1999: 156). We would certainly find this perplexing, as performance of such an act would be incompatible with having the virtue. But the example offers no support for her claim that we would (or should) feel puzzled when someone to whom we ascribed one virtue fell down in respect of a quite different virtue.

6   Note that this picture comes under pressure too from the "situationist" critique of traditional views of virtues as dispositions. See above, Chapter 2, note 5.

SIX   COURAGE: AN OUTDATED VIRTUE?

1   It is true that someone who has once failed in courage and is determined to redeem himself may be less concerned about the identity of the cause he takes up for this purpose than about its capacity to test him. But if redemption is to be complete, there needs to be resemblance between the old cause and the new one. A soldier who has run away on the battlefield will restore his self-esteem more effectively by forcing himself to stand his ground on another battlefield than by becoming a Hollywood stuntman.

2   I ignore here the much-vaunted (by politicians) risk of terrorist attack. As the actuarial calculations of insurance firms confirm, the objective probability of being murdered in a terrorist "incident" in the USA or UK is vastly smaller than that of being killed in a road accident.

3   Some might think that the three theological virtues of faith, hope and charity would be useful too – along with a considerable injection of divine aid.

4   The eighteenth-century American revivalist preacher Jonathan Edward's portrayal of hell is less lurid but no less frightening than medieval representations of the plight of the damned. Edwards focuses on the pitilessness of God at the Last Judgement: "Then the Judge will deal in fury: his eye shall not spare, neither will he have pity: and though ye cry

in a loud voice, yet will he not hear you. . . . The wrath of God will be poured out upon the wicked without mixture, and vengeance will have its full weight" (Edwards 1788: 184). One would have needed courage in spades to believe this and not give in to hopelessness.

5   This reconstruction, however, needs to avoid the solipsism which can all too easily infect "authentic" attempts at value creation. If everyone creates his own values, then every individual is in danger of living in a moral universe of his own. Perhaps Nietzsche would hold that the superior being (the *Übermensch*), should joyfully and courageously embrace such splendid moral isolation. Yet, to make a point familiar to Wittgensteinians, the rejection of any external standards from which his value judgements can be criticised makes it doubtful whether he can attach even subjective meaning to "right" and "wrong," in the absence of any independently verifiable criteria of the application of those words. The Nietzschean "overman" may therefore have moved not only beyond conventional good and evil but out of the realm of intelligible value talk altogether.

Bibliography

This Bibliography lists all titles referred to in the text plus a selection of further useful reading.

Aquinas, St Thomas (1966) *Summa Theologiae*, vol. 42: *Courage*, trans. Anthony Ross and P. G. Walsh, Oxford, London and New York: Blackfriars, in conjunction with Eyre & Spottiswoode and McGraw-Hill.

—— (1967) *Summa Theologiae*, vol. 19: *The Emotions*, trans. Eric D'Arcy, Oxford, London and New York: Blackfriars, in conjunction with Eyre & Spottiswoode and McGraw-Hill.

—— (1970) *Summa Theologiae*, vol. 11: *Man*, trans. Timothy Suttor, Oxford, London and New York: Blackfriars, in conjunction with Eyre & Spottiswoode and McGraw-Hill.

—— (2005) *The Cardinal Virtues: Prudence, Justice, Fortitude, and Temperance*, trans., edited by Richard J. Regan, Indianapolis: Hackett.

Aristotle (1905) *Politics*, trans. B. Jowett, Oxford: Clarendon Press.

—— (1954) *Nicomachean Ethics*, trans. D. Ross, Oxford: Oxford University Press.

Austen, Jane (1986) *Persuasion*, London: Buccaneer Books.

Badhwar, Neera K. (1996) "The Limited Unity of Virtue," *Noûs* 30: 306–29.

Bauhn, Per (2003) *The Value of Courage*, Lund: Nordic Academic Press.

Berlin, Isaiah (1969) "Two Concepts of Liberty," *Four Essays on Liberty*, London: Oxford University Press, pp. 118–72.

Brady, Michelle E. (2005) "The Fearlessness of Courage," *Southern Journal of Philosophy* 43: 189–211.

Brown, Gordon (2007) *Courage: Eight Portraits*, London: Bloomsbury.

Bryson, Bill (2004) *A Short History of Nearly Everything*, London: Black Swan.

Burnet, Gilbert (1684) *The Abridgment of the History of the Reformation of the Church of England*, 2nd edn, London: Richard Chiswell.

Callan, Eamonn (2005) "Patience and Courage," in C. Williams (ed.) *Personal Virtues: Introductory Essays*, Basingstoke: Palgrave Macmillan, pp. 202–21.

Cicero, Marcus Tullius (1961) *De Officiis*, trans. W. Miller, Cambridge, MA: Harvard University Press; and London: William Heinemann.

Conrad, Joseph (1949) *Lord Jim*, Harmondsworth: Penguin.

Crane, Stephen (2008) *The Red Badge of Courage*, edited by D. Pizer and E. C. Link, 4th edn, New York and London: W. W. Norton & Co.

De Young, Rebecca (2003) "Power Made Perfect in Weakness: Aquinas's Transformation of the Virtue of Courage," *Medieval Philosophy and Theology* 11: 147–80.

Dickens, Charles (1985) *Oliver Twist*, New York: Avenel.

Doris, John M. (2002) *Lack of Character: Personality and Moral Behavior*, Cambridge and New York: Cambridge University Press.

—— (2005) "Replies: Evidence and Sensibility," *Philosophy and Phenomenological Research* 71: 656–77.

Dryden, John (1697) "Dedication to the Right Honourable Charles Earl of Dorset and Middlesex," in *The Satires of Decimus Junius Juvenal Translated into English Verse*, 2nd edn, London: Jacob Tonson.

Duff, Antony (1987) "Aristotelian Courage," *Ratio* 29: 2–15.

Dumbach, Annette and Newborn, Jud (2006) *Sophie Scholl and the White Rose*, Oxford: Oneworld.

Edgeworth, Mary (1986 [1801]) *Belinda*, London and New York: Pandora.

Edwards, Jonathan (1788) *Practical Sermons Never Before Published*, Edinburgh: M. Gray.

Eliot, T. S. (1961) *Selected Poems*, London: Faber & Faber.

Epictetus (1983) *Handbook* [*Enchiridion*], trans. Nicholas White, Indianapolis: Hackett.

Eustachius a Sancto Paulo (1677) *Ethica sive Summa Moralis Disciplinae*, London: J. Redmayne.

Farthing, G. William (2005) "Attitudes towards Heroic and Nonheroic Risk Takers as Mates and as Friends," *Evolution and Human Behavior* 26: 171–85.

Faunce, T., Bolsin, S. and Chan, W.-P. (2004) "Supporting Whistleblowers in Academic Medicine: Training and Respecting the Courage of Professional Conscience," *Journal of Medical Ethics* 30: 40–3.

Flegal, A. Russell (1998) "Clair Patterson's Influence on Environmental Research," *Environmental Research*, Section A, 78: 65–70.

Foot, Philippa (2002) *Virtues and Vices and Other Essays in Moral Philosophy*, new edn, Oxford: Clarendon Press.

Garden, Timothy (2001) Review of *The Mystery of Courage*, by William I. Miller, *Times Higher Education Supplement*, 27 Apr. Available at Tim Garden's webpage, <http://www.tgarden.demon.co.uk/writings/articles/2001/010427thes.html>

Geach, Peter (1977) *The Virtues*, Cambridge: Cambridge University Press.

Griswold, Charles L., Jr (1986) "Philosophy, Education, and Courage in Plato's *Laches*," *Interpretation* 14: 177–93.

Hamilton, Mary Agnes (1925) *Mary Macarthur*, London: Leonard Parsons.

Harman, Gilbert (1999–2000) "Moral Philosophy Meets Social Psychology: Virtue Ethics and the Fundamental Attribution Error," *Proceedings of the Aristotelian Society* 99: 315–51.

Heidegger, Martin (1962) *Being and Time*, trans. J. Macquarrie and E. Robinson, Oxford: Blackwell.

Herbert, George (1961) *The Poems of George Herbert*, Oxford: Oxford University Press.

Hobbs, Angela (2000) *Plato and the Hero: Courage, Manliness and the Impersonal Good*, Cambridge: Cambridge University Press.

Hopkin, Michael (2004) "Mice Yield Secret of Maternal Courage," *Nature News*, at K8 Science, BioEd Online, Baylor College of Medicine. <http://www.k8science.org/news/news.cfm?art=1106>

Hunt, Lester H. (1980) "Courage and Principle," *Canadian Journal of Philosophy* 10: 281–93.

Hursthouse, Rosalind (1999) *On Virtue Ethics*, Oxford: Oxford University Press.

Kamtekar, Rachana (2004) "Situationism and Virtue Ethics on the Content of Our Character," *Ethics* 114: 458–91.

Kant, Immanuel (1909) *Fundamental Principles of the Metaphysic of Morals*, in *Critique of Practical Reason and Other Works in the Theory of Ethics*, trans. T. K. Abbott, London: Longmans.

Kennedy, John F. (1964) *Profiles in Courage*, New York: Harper & Row.

[Kennedy, John F.] (2008) John F. Kennedy Presidential Library and Museum website. <http://www.jfklibrary.org>

Kipling, Rudyard (1963) *A Choice of Kipling's Verse*, edited by T. S. Eliot, London and Boston: Faber & Faber.

Bibliography

Kochanska, G. (1991) "Socialization and Temperament in the Development of Guilt and Conscience," *Child Development* 62: 1379–92.

La Rochefoucauld, F., Duc de (1786) *Maxims and Moral Reflections*. London: Lockyer Davis.

Lear, Jonathan (2006) *Radical Hope: Ethics in the Face of Cultural Devastation*, Cambridge, MA, and London: Harvard University Press.

Locke, John (1705) *Some Thoughts Concerning Education*, 5th edn, rev., London: A. & J. Churchill.

Lovibond, Sabina (1983) *Realism and Imagination in Ethics*, Minneapolis: University of Minnesota Press.

Lykken, D.T. (1982) "Fearlessness," *Psychology Today* (Sep): 23–6.

Macaulay, Thomas Babington, Baron (1897) "Horatius: A Lay Made about the Year of the City CCCLX," in *The Life and Works of Lord Macaulay*, London: Longmans, Green, vol. 9, pp. 466–84.

MacCulloch, Diarmaid (1996) *Thomas Cranmer: A Life*, New Haven, CT, and London: Yale University Press.

MacIntyre, Alasdair (1984) *After Virtue*, 2nd edn, London: Duckworth.

—— (1999) *Dependent Rational Animals: Why Human Beings Need the Virtues*, Chicago and La Salle, IL: Open Court.

Mackenzie, Compton (1962) *Certain Aspects of Moral Courage*, New York: Doubleday & Co.

Mansfield, Harvey C. (2006) *Manliness*, New Haven, CT, and London: Yale University Press.

Marcus Aurelius (1964) *Meditations*, trans. Maxwell Staniforth, Harmondsworth: Penguin.

Mayhew, Henry (1987) *Mayhew's London Underworld*, edited, selected by P. Quennell, London: Century.

McCain, John (2004) *Why Courage Matters*, New York: Random House.

McFeely, William S. (1982) *Grant: A Biography*, New York and London: W. W. Norton & Co.

McLynn, Frank (2004) *1759: The Year Britain became Master of the World*, London: Jonathan Cape.

Mill, John Stuart (1910) *On Liberty in Utilitarianism, Liberty and Representative Government*, London: Everyman's Library.

Miller, William Ian (2000) *The Mystery of Courage*, Cambridge, MA, and London: Harvard University Press.

Montaigne, M. de (1987) "On Constancy," in *The Complete Essays*, trans., edited by M. A. Screech, Harmondsworth: Penguin, pp. 47–9.

Mora, Alberto (2006) "Acceptance Speech," John F. Kennedy Library and Museum website. <http://www.jfklibrary.org/Education+and+Public+Programs/Profile+in+courage+Award/Award+Recipients/Alberto+Mora/Acceptance+Speech+by+Alberto+Mora.htm>

—— (2008) "Statement to the Senate Committee on Armed Services Hearing on the Treatment of Detainees in U.S. Custody," United States Senate Armed Services Committee website. <http://armed-services.senate.gov/statemnt/2008/June/Mora%2006–17–08.pdf>.

Needleman, Herbert L. (1998) "Clair Patterson and Robert Kehoe: Two Views on Lead Toxicity," *Environmental Research*, Section A, 78: 79–85.

Nicolson, Juliet (2006) *The Perfect Summer: Dancing into Shadow in 1911*, London: John Murray.

Nielsen, Kai (2000) "Death and the Meaning of Life," in E. D. Klemke (ed.) *The Meaning of Life*, Oxford: Oxford University Press, 153–9.

Nietzsche, Friedrich (1961) *Thus Spake Zarathustra*, trans. R. J. Hollingdale, Harmondsworth: Penguin.

—— (1968) *The Will to Power*, trans. Walter Kaufmann and R. J. Hollingdale, New York: Vintage Books.

Nozick, Robert (1981) *Philosophical Explanations*, Oxford: Clarendon Press.

Nriagu, Jerome O. (1998) "Clair Patterson and Robert Kehoe's Paradigm of 'Show Me the Data' on Environmental Lead Poisoning," *Environmental Research*, Section A, 78: 71–8.

Oderberg, David S. (1999) "On the Cardinality of the Cardinal Virtues," *International Journal of Philosophical Studies* 7: 305–22.

Oliner, Samuel P. and Oliner, Pearl M. (1988) *The Altruistic Personality: Rescuers of Jews in Nazi Europe*, New York: Free Press.

Orr, Emma Restall (2007) *Living with Honour: A Pagan Ethics*, Winchester, UK, and Washington: O Books.

Owen, Wilfred (1973) *War Poems and Others*, edited by Dominic Hibberd, London: Chatto & Windus.

Peterson, Christopher and Seligman, Martin E. P. (2004) *Character Strengths and Virtues: A Handbook and Classification*, Washington, DC, and Oxford: American Psychological Association and Oxford University Press.

Pieper, Josef (1966) *The Four Cardinal Virtues*, Notre Dame, IN: University of Notre Dame Press.

Plato (1953a) *Laches*, in *The Dialogues of Plato*, trans. Benjamin Jowett, 4th edn, Oxford: Clarendon Press, vol. 1, pp. 67–102.

—— (1953b) *Republic*, in *The Dialogues of Plato*, trans. Benjamin Jowett, 4th edn, Oxford: Clarendon Press, vol. 2, pp. 1–499.

—— (1953c) *Statesman*, in *The Dialogues of Plato*, trans. Benjamin Jowett, 4th edn, Oxford: Clarendon Press, vol. 2, pp. 429–530.

Plutarch (1821) "Life of Cato the Younger," in *Plutarch's Lives*, trans. J. and W. Langhorn, London: J. Richardson, vol. 6, pp. 234–311.

Poland, Warren S. (2007) "Clinician's Corner: Courage and Morals," *American Imago* 64: 253–9.

Pollard, A. F. (1906) *Thomas Cranmer and the English Reformation 1489–1556*, New York and London: Putnam's Sons.

Putman, Daniel (1997) "Psychological Courage," *Philosophy, Psychiatry, and Psychology* 4: 1–11.

—— (2001) "The Emotions of Courage," *Journal of Social Philosophy* 32: 463–70.

Rabbås, Øyvind (2003) "Definitions and Paradigms: Laches' First Definition," *Phronesis* 69: 143–68.

Rawls, John (1972) *A Theory of Justice*, London, Oxford and New York: Oxford University Press.

Rhodes, R. and Strain, J. J. (2004) "Whistleblowing in Academic Medicine," *Journal of Medical Ethics* 30: 35–9.

Ridley, Matt (1997) *The Origins of Virtue*, London: Penguin.

Rogers, Kelly (1994) "Aristotle on the Motive of Courage," *Southern Journal of Philosophy* 32: 303–13.

Rorty, Amélie Oksenberg (1988) "The Two Faces of Courage," in *Mind in Action: Essays in the Philosophy of Mind*, Boston: Beacon Press, pp. 299–313.

Rosen, Ralph M. and Sluiter, Ineka (2003) *Andreia: Studies in Manliness and Courage in Classical Antiquity*, Leiden: Brill.

Salgado, Gamini (1977) *The Elizabethan Underworld*, London: Dent.

Saltaris, Christina (2002) "Psychopathy in Juvenile Offenders: Can Temperament and Attachment Be Considered as Robust Developmental Precursors?" *Clinical Psychology Review* 22: 729–52.

Schmid, Walter T. (1992) *On Manly Courage: A Study of Plato's Laches*, Carbondale and Edwardsville: Southern Illinois University Press.

Schopenhauer, Arthur (1970) *Essays and Aphorisms*, trans. R. J. Hollingdale, Harmondsworth: Penguin.

Seneca (2005) *On Tranquillity of Mind*, in *Dialogues and Letters*, trans., edited by
 C. D. N. Costa, Harmondsworth: Penguin, pp. 29–58.

Sherman, Nancy (2005) *Stoic Warriors: The Ancient Philosophy Behind the Military
 Mind*, Oxford: Oxford University Press.

Sherman, William Tecumseh (1990) *Memoirs of William Tecumseh Sherman*,
 New York: Library of America.

Sidgwick, Henry (1907) *The Methods of Ethics*, 7th edn, London: Macmillan.

Staub, Erwin (1978–9) *Positive Social Behavior and Morality*, New York: Academic
 Press.

Taylor, Charles (2007) "A Different Kind of Courage" [review of Jonathan
 Lear, *Radical Hope*], *New York Review of Books* 54, no. 7: 4–8.

Thucydides (1994) *The History of the Peloponnesian War*, trans. Benjamin Jowett,
 edited by Chris Scarre, London: Folio Society.

Tillich, Paul (2000) *The Courage to Be*, 2nd edn, New Haven, CT, and London:
 Yale University Press.

Trivers, Robert L. (1971) "On the evolution of reciprocal altruism,"
 Quarterly Review of Biology 46: 35–57.

van Vliederhoven, Gerard (2008) *Cordiale de Quattuor Novissimis* [Heartsease
 concerning the four last things], trans. Richard Byrn, Richard Byrn's
 homepage. <http://richardbyrn.co.uk/cordiale.htm>

Velleman, J. David (1992) "What Happens When Someone Acts?" *Mind*
 101: 461–81.

von Wright, Georg Henrik (1963) *The Varieties of Goodness*, London: Routledge
 & Kegan Paul.

Wagner, Richard (1960) *Siegfried*, Opera libretto, New York and London:
 G. Schirmer.

Wallace, James D. (1978) *Virtues and Vices*, Ithaca, NY, and London: Cornell
 University Press.

Walton, Douglas N. (1986) *Courage: A Philosophical Investigation*, Berkeley, Los
 Angeles and London: University of California Press.

—— (1990) "Courage, Relativism and Practical Reasoning," *Philosophia* 20:
 227–40.

Wattles, Jeffrey (2005) "Towards a Phenomenology of Courageous Willing,"
 Analecta Husserliana 84: 81–95.

Yeats, W. B. (1950) *The Collected Poems of W. B. Yeats*, 2nd edn, London:
 Macmillan & Co.

Index

akrasia (weakness of will) 53–4, 59
andreia (manliness) 11, 65, 70
Antigone 70
Aquinas, St Thomas 2, 3, 51–2, 54–5, 79–81, 82, 84, 93–4
Aristotle 3, 5, 6–11, 17, 20, 27, 31, 32–5, 37, 64, 66, 67, 71, 90, 107–8, 109, 111, 126, 128, 159n3, 160n1, 162n2, 164n1
Asperger's Syndrome 19
Aurelius, Marcus (Emperor) 96, 163n7
Auschwitz 91
Austen, Jane 91–2
Austin, J.L. 103, 164n12

Bauhn, Per 116, 118–20
Being and Time (Heidegger) 151
Bernstein, Leonard 132
Bolsin, S. 146
bravery *see* courage
Brown, Gordon 108, 160n9
Bryson, Bill 148–9
Burnet, Gilbert 59
Bushido 129

Callan, Eamonn 72, 96
Calvinism 154
Canus, Julius 102–3, 106
cardinal virtue 2–3, 84, 114, 144 (*see also* courage as a virtue)
Cato the Younger 98–9
Chan, W.-P. 146
Churchill, Sir Winston 2–3, 124
Cicero, Marcus Tullius 113–14

Civil War, US 18, 104, 111–12, 137–9
Clausewitz, Carl von 63
Conrad, Joseph 92
conscientious objectors 63–4
Constancie (Herbert) 158
continence 6–11, 18
corticotropin-releasing hormone (CRH) 76
costly signalling theory (CST) 76–8
courage: "abstractionist view" of 117–18, 120; and autonomy 39–40; in children 85; cultural variations 5, 12–13, 129; and explanation of action 41–6; and fear of hell 153–4, 165n4; and fearlessness 14–21, 37–8; and good ends Ch.5 *passim*; and manliness Ch.3 *passim* 162n1, 162n2; and the loss of meaning 149–53; in modern world 140–4; moral 21–7, 146, 156; "psychological" 19; and risk-taking 75–9; its scope and varieties 3–5, 81, 142; and reason 11–14, 49–50, 133; as a virtue 2–3, 6–11, 32–5, 79–81, Ch.5 *passim* 137 (*see also* cardinal virtue); and spirit 51–2, 55; and will 48–56; *see also* fortitude
cowardice 4, 122, 150, 157
Crane, Stephen 137, 158
Cranmer, Thomas (Archbishop) 56–61
Crow tribe (North America) 12–13, 129, 142

Dickens, Charles 68–9
Doris, John 161n5

Dryden, John 163n2
"Dunkirk spirit" 62

Edgeworth, Mary 107
Edwards, Jonathan 165n4
"Eleatic Stranger" 113
Eliot, T.S. 30, 152
Epictetus 97–8
Ethyl Corporation (US) 146–9
Eustachius a Sancto Paulo 79

Farthing, G. William 76–8
Faunce, T. 146
Feldernhalle (Munich) 1, 3
feminism 68
fortitude: contrasted with courage
    82–6; contrasted with patience 93–7,
    163n2; in modern age 140; and
    personal narratives 89–93; Stoic
    views of 96–100, 102–3, 163n7; role
    in sustaining self 86–93
Foot, Philippa 115, 119, 121–24

Garden, Sir Timothy 19
Geach, Peter 115
global warming 143–4
Gordon, Charles George (General) 98
Götterdämmerung (Wagner) 21
Graf, Willi 1, 3, 14
Grant, Ulysses S. (General) 104–6
Guantánamo Bay naval base (Cuba)
    23–4
Gulag (Soviet Union) 26–7

Harman, Gilbert 161n5
Heidegger, Martin 151
Hemingway, Ernest 23
Herbert, George 158
Horatius (Roman hero) 62
Hursthouse, Rosalind 126–8, 165n5

If (Kipling) 98, 99–100, 164n9

Jesus Christ 88
Jews, rescuers of 43–6, 161n5

John F. Kennedy Library Foundation 23
justice 144

Kant, Immanuel 9, 115, 117, 124
Kehoe, Robert Arthur 147
Kennedy, John F. (US President) 23,
    111–12, 116
Kipling, Rudyard 98, 99–100
Kochanska, G. 16
Kolbe, Maximilian 91

Laches (Plato) 66–7, 112–13, 126, 133
Lear, Jonathan 12–13, 75, 78–9, 108,
    142
Locke, John 84–6, 95
Lord Jim (Conrad) 92
Lovibond, Sabina 68
Lykken, D.T. 16

Macarthur, Mary 73–5
Macaulay, Thomas Babington 62
Macbeth 48, 52–3, 56
Macbeth, Lady 48–9, 56
McCain, John 159n4, 160n9
MacIntyre, Alasdair 89
Mandela, Nelson 141
Mansfield, Harvey 65
Mary I, Queen 57–9
Mercutio 130–3
"methodological disdain" 101–3
Mill, John Stuart 156–7
Miller, William Ian 11–12, 14, 22, 116,
    117–18, 120, 130, 32
Mime (dwarf) 16–17, 21
Mora, Alberto J. 23–4, 25

Nietzsche, Friedrich 138, 141, 149–51,
    152, 155, 166n5
Nozick, Robert 45

Oliner, Samuel and Pearl 43–6, 48, 56
Oliver Twist (Dickens) 68–9
On Liberty (Mill) 156–7
"On tranquillity of mind" (Seneca)
    102–3

Orr, Emma Restall 140
Owen, Wilfred 63, 67

patience 68–74, 93–7
Patterson, Clair 146–9
Peloponnesian War 69
Pericles 69–71, 81, 162n3
Persuasion (Austen) 91–3
Peter, St. 68
Peterson, Christopher 6–7
Pieper, Josef 114
Plato 5, 12, 20, 66–7, 112–13, 125, 133, 140
Plenty Coups (Crow chief) 142
Plutarch 98–9
Poland, Warren 36
Pollard, A.F. 60
"prisoner's dilemma" 143–4
Probst, Christoph 13
Profile in Courage Award 23–4
prudence 119, 144, 158
Putman, Daniel 19, 116

Rawls, John 110
Red Badge of Courage, The (Crane) 137–9
Rhodes, R 145
Richard III, King 118, 120
Ring of the Nibelung, The (Wagner) 16
Rochefoucauld, Duke de la 4, 30–1, 32, 65, 101
Romeo and Juliet (Shakespeare) 130–3
Rorty, Amélie 41–2, 46, 64–5, 125, 127–8, 130

Saltaris, Christina 16
Schmorell, Alex 1, 3, 14
Scholl, Hans 1, 3, 14
Scholl, Sophie 81, 111, 136
Schopenhauer, Arthur 115
Seligman, Martin E.P. 6–7
Seneca, Lucius Annaeus 102–3
Shakespeare, William 132 (*see also* Macbeth, Lady Macbeth, Mercutio, *Romeo and Juliet*)

Sherman, Nancy 97
Sherman, William Tecumseh 18
Sidgwick, Henry 22, 83
Siegfried (hero) 14, 16–18, 20–1, 37, 160n7
situationism 161n5
Socrates 66–7, 133
Spinoza, Baruch (Benedict de) 88
Statesman (Plato) 113, 125
Staub, Ervin 43, 162n4
Stephen, James Fitzjames 21–2, 25
Stoicism *see* fortitude, Stoic views of
Strain, J.J. 145

temperance 113, 125, 140, 144
tetraethyl lead (TEL), campaign to ban 146–9
thumos (spirit) 20
Tillich, Paul 87–8, 114, 150–1
Townshend, George (Brigadier) 99

Velleman, J. David 49–55
Van Vliederhoven, Gerard 154
virtue 6–11, 31, 100, 107–8;
    expansiveness of (Rorty) 125–6;
    male and female Ch.3 *passim*;
    "operating as a virtue" (Foot) 122–4;
    unity of the virtues thesis 124–8 (*see also* cardinal virtue, continence)
Von Wright, G.H. 115

Wagner, Richard 16–17
Wallace, James 115–16, 117–18, 120, 130, 132
Walton, Douglas 114
"war against terror" 155
Waste Land, The (Eliot) 152
Wayne, John 14, 18, 37–8
West Side Story (Bernstein) 132–3
whistle-blowing 145–9
White Rose group 1, 13–14, 81
will *see* courage and will (*see also* akrasia)
World War I 63–4, 66, 74

Yeats, W.B. 155

Related titles from Routledge

Moral Epistemology –
'New Problems of Philosophy'
Aaron Zimmerman

How do we know right from wrong? Do we even have moral knowledge? Moral epistemology studies these and related questions about our understanding of virtue and vice. It is one of philosophy's perennial problems, and has recently been the subject of intense debate as a result of findings in developmental and social psychology.

In this outstanding introduction to the subject Aaron Zimmerman covers the following key topics:

- What is moral epistemology? What are its methods?
- Skepticism about moral knowledge based on the anthropological record of deep and persistent moral disagreement, including contextualism
- Moral nihilism, including debates concerning God and morality and the relation between moral knowledge and our motives and reasons to act morally
- Epistemic moral scepticism, intuitionism and the possibility of inferring 'ought' from 'is,' discussing Locke, Hume, Kant, Audi, and many others
- How children acquire moral concepts and become more reliable judges
- Criticisms of those who would reduce moral knowledge to value-neutral knowledge or attempt to replace moral belief with emotion.

Throughout the book Zimmerman argues that our belief in moral knowledge can survive sceptical challenges. He also draws on a rich range of examples from Plato's Meno and Dickens's David Copperfield to Bernard Madoff and Saddam Hussein.

Including chapter summaries and annotated further reading at the end of each chapter, *Moral Epistemology* is essential reading for all students of ethics, epistemology and moral psychology.

ISBN 13: 978–0–415–48553–1 (hbk)
ISBN 13: 978–0–415–48554–8 (pbk)
ISBN 13: 978–0–203–85086–2 (ebk)

Available at all good bookshops
For ordering and further information please visit:
www.routledge.com

Related titles from Routledge

The Routledge Companion to Ethics
Edited by John Skorupski

'Written by leaders in the field, and with depth as well as breadth, this is the ideal companion for anyone with an interest in philosophical ethics'
– *Roger Crisp, St. Anne's College, Oxford*

The Routledge Companion to Ethics is an outstanding survey of the whole field of ethics by a distinguished international team of contributors. Over sixty entries are divided into six clear sections:

- the history of ethics
- meta-ethics
- perspectives from outside ethics
- perspectives in ethics
- morality
- debates in ethics.

The Routledge Companion to Ethics is a superb resource for anyone interested in the subject, whether in philosophy or related subjects such as politics, education, or law. Fully indexed and cross-referenced, with helpful further reading sections at the end of each entry, it is ideal for those coming to the field of ethics for the first time as well as readers already familiar with the subject.

ISBN 13: 978–0–415–41362–6 (hbk)
ISBN 13: 978–0–203–85070–1 (ebk)

Available at all good bookshops
For ordering and further information please visit:
www.routledge.com

Related titles from Routledge

On Delusion
Jennifer Radden

'Immensely welcome, erudite and informative, this book is a significant contribution to not just topically inventive pedagogy, but to literature on the puzzles, poignancies, and quandaries of delusion.' – *George Graham, author of The Disordered Mind: An Introduction to Philosophy of Mind and Mental Illness*

'A clearly written and accessible but also interesting and original account of many of the core issues surrounding delusions.' – *Lisa Bortolotti, Birmingham University*

Delusions play a fundamental role in the history of psychology, philosophy and culture, dividing not only the mad from the sane but reason from unreason. Yet the very nature and extent of delusions are poorly understood. What are delusions? How do they differ from everyday errors or mistaken beliefs? Are they scientific categories?

In this superb, panoramic investigation of delusion Jennifer Radden explores these questions and more, unravelling a fascinating story that ranges from Descartes's demon to famous first-hand accounts of delusion, such as Daniel Schreber's *Memoirs of My Nervous Illness*.

Radden places delusion in both a clinical and cultural context and explores a fascinating range of themes: delusions as both individually and collectively held, including the phenomenon of *folies á deux*; spiritual and religious delusions, in particular what distinguishes normal religious belief from delusions with religious themes; how we assess those suffering from delusion from a moral standpoint; and how we are to interpret violent actions when they are the result of delusional thinking. As well as more common delusions, such as those of grandeur, she also discusses some of the most interesting and perplexing forms of clinical delusion, such as Cotard and Capgras.

Jennifer Radden is Professor of Philosophy and a former Chair of Philosophy at the University of Massachusetts, Boston.

Hbk ISBN 13: 978–0–415–77447–5
Pbk ISBN 13: 978–0–415–77448–2
Ebk ISBN 13: 978–0–203–84651–3

Available at all good bookshops
For ordering and further information please visit:
www.routledge.com